# I'll Give It Six Months

*Memoirs of a lucky man*

Robert Howe

Copyright © 2018 Robert Howe

All rights reserved, including the right to reproduce this book, or portions thereof, in any form. No part of this text may be reproduced, transmitted, downloaded, decompiled, reverse engineered, or stored in any form, or introduced into any information storage and retrieval system in any form or by any means, whether electronic or mechanical, without the express written permission of the author.

The views expressed in this work are solely those of the author and do not necessarily reflect the views of the publisher, and the publisher hereby disclaims any responsibility for them.

ISBN: 978-0-244-66904-1
*Paperback version*


PublishNation
www.publishnation.co.uk

# Introduction

Having had a number of diverse occupations, I have met some very interesting and famous people during my life. I was born in a hospital next to Wormwood Scrubs in 1942 and my upbringing in West London mirrored that of the MP Alan Johnson as we lived only streets apart. Apprentice to William Luff, the UK's greatest violin maker, I joined the Merchant Navy at twenty and saw most of the world. I was a butcher/cook at St George's Hospital and also a Student Theatre Technician at Guy's Hospital before taking the Civil Service entrance exam. I joined the Board of Trade before being promoted to Chief Photo Printer and moving to the Department of Employment in Cheshire. I became an Immigration Officer based at Manchester Airport with the Home Office and have worked at Heathrow and Liverpool. I seconded to the Diplomatic Service and was posted to West Africa during my Civil Service career. I have had many conversations with some very famous people, including Omar Sharif and Rudolf Nureyev, as well as a few arguments with MPs and pop stars. On retirement, I became a trustee with a local Riding for the Disabled group.

It has taken me two years to put together this collection of memories and I have gained an enormous amount of pleasure and satisfaction in writing them. In doing so, I have remembered old friends and times almost forgotten, and I can honestly say that that alone has been worth the effort. If anyone reads the book, I hope they enjoy it and perhaps are tempted to put their own life down in print. It's great therapy and a lot of fun.

To the best of my memory, all characters and events in this book are truthfully recorded, but memory dims over the years and I must apologise to family and friends if I have the odd detail not quite as it happened. I am also mindful of the Official Secrets Act, which I hope I haven't contravened, as to the best of my knowledge all relevant episodes recorded are in the public domain.

*Dedicated to my wonderful wife, Linda,*
*who has put up with me for the past forty-six years*
*and without whom my life would have been unthinkable.*

\*\*\*

# Contents

*Me, but who's my tailor?*

# Chapter 1

## *A Maternity Room with a View*

I first saw the light of day on 11 August 1942 at some time just after eight o'clock in the morning. Being the third child born in the family, I'm told that my entry into the world was without too much drama and that I weighed a healthy 8lbs 4oz. The venue for my entry into the Howe family was at Hammersmith Hospital, Du Cane Road, West London, which is situated right next to HMP Wormwood Scrubs. I don't think that my mother, Caroline, thought this was an omen of doom; in fact, we both returned to Du Cane Road many years later accompanied by my aunt, Peg, to attend a carol service in the prison itself. I seem to recall that the service and the carols took second place to the more interesting game of "spot the murderer".

Of course, in 1942 the war was still raging and my father, Robert, was nowhere to be seen, preferring to be enjoying himself eating pasta and killing Germans in Italy. It would be almost three years until I met the man who was my lovely dad and I believe I kept asking my mother who he was and when would he be leaving. My first home was a flat in Oswin House, a small block somewhere in Shepherd's Bush and near where my mother worked during the war as a cook in a club called The Feathers. The Feathers Clubs Association was founded in 1934 by Mrs Freda Dudley Ward, who was reputed to have set up the association at the behest of the Prince of Wales, who allowed his crest of the three feathers to be used as the insignia of the association, from which the name of the charity derives. Initially formed to aid those suffering in the Depression of the 1930s, the Feathers Association moved into youth and community work after the Second World War.

Oswin House, which I think was in Poynter Street, London, W11, but I have been unable to find it on present day maps, was very near the railway tracks and as such, a favourite for Mr Goering's Luftwaffe, and as a consequence it was always having its windows caved in. My sister Pat, who was ten at this time, has told me that on one occasion during an air raid the blast that took the windows out also jammed the front door firmly shut and the three of us were trapped until the overworked fire brigade could free us, and on another raid my cot was covered in glass from the windows with me underneath but without a single scratch.

With all this carnage happening in London, my mother made the sensible decision to move out of London for a while and return with us to her mother's home in Northumberland. The memory I have of these trips north to Seaton Delaval are of a fearsome grandmother who was a staunch chapelgoer and even fiercer supporter of the Labour Party. My grandmother, Margaret, was married twice; first to a Mr Golightly, and when he died she married a Sidney Proudfoot, and they lived at Foremans Row, Seaton Delaval.

My father used to tease my mother by saying that with names like these she must have some Red Indian blood in her veins. Grandmother always said that she could never forgive Winston Churchill for forcing the Northumberland miners to return to work during the national strike, one of whom was my grandfather, Sidney. In 1926, the coal miner's union leaders finally announced that at the end of the current contract they would call a nationwide strike unless they were granted what amounted to a substantial increase in pay with an hour less on the day. The contract ended. They duly presented their demands, which the mine owners rejected.

My sister Pat always says that this was a difficult time for her because when at school in Seaton Delaval she was a Cockney with a funny accent and on her return to London was a Geordie also with a peculiar way of talking.

A family legend, and one I'm not sure I should have included, was that while I was staying in Northumberland with my grandparents (and I only have my mother's word for this) I was prone to asking various visitors and family members "Would you like me to dance for you?". My mother was convinced that I would grow up to be a dancer. Perhaps I should have pursued that path—I quite fancy changing my name to Robertov Howeski—but asthma as a child stopped any thought of my name in lights over the Royal Opera House in Covent Garden.

The place-name "Seaton Delaval" was first attested as "Seton de la Val" in 1270. "Seaton" simply means "sea town", referring to the village's nearness to the North Sea. The land was held by the de la Val family, who took their name from Le Val in Normandy. The folk song "Blackleg Miner" mentions the village.

*Oh, Delaval is a terrible place*
*They rub wet clay in the blackleg's face.*
*And around the heaps they run a foot race,*
*To catch the blackleg miner!*
*So dinna gan near the Seghill mine.*
*Across way they stretch a line,*
*To catch the throat and break the spine*
*Of the dirty blackleg miner!*

In 1946 the war ended, my father returned, and the family found ourselves living at 31 Winterbourne House, Portland Road, W11.

Portland Road, where Winterbourne House is located, was built in 1850 in today's Notting Hill, and was once one of London's worst slums. The street is actually made up of two streets broken east-west. The smart Ladbroke Estate was constructed alongside the much more downmarket Norland Estate, home at the time of its construction to piggeries and potteries, alongside a gypsy encampment. The Ladbroke Estate was always intended for prosperous, servant-keeping professionals, but today it houses the super-rich: bankers and foreign property investors.

Dad got a job working for the Alfred Dunhill Company at their factory in Cumberland Road, Plaistow, as an electrician's mate, and life began to return to something approaching normal. My father was a clever man who had been stopped by his father from taking up a scholarship at the Grey Coats School. He was also a very shy man who hated fuss and didn't like going to cafés and hardly ever went to a pub; however, at the children's Christmas party that Dunhill gave for the staff every year, he took centre stage, dressed up in a tail coat, false moustache, and fake bald head to play "the great Simpreni: master magician". I couldn't believe that this was my dad up there but was so proud that it was. I remember one time the electrician who Dad worked with and who lived on Canvey Island came to stay with us because on the night of 31 January 1953 a tidal surge came down the North Sea, flooding low-lying lands in its path. Canvey Island was badly hit with the sea wall being washed away. Fifty-eight people lost their lives and the island was evacuated, including Percy, the electrician. Only at the end of his life did I start to appreciate how hard my dad worked to put food on the table and provide a stable home. We always had a summer holiday somewhere on the south coast, usually in a caravan in Leysdown-on-Sea, Kent, sometimes in a B&B, and there were always presents on birthdays and at Christmas.

The holidays in Leysdown were great as some of my cousins were there at the same time and, on occasion, my mad uncle Griff. Griff was married to my dad's sister, Lilly, and he was more of a kid than any of us, with his cry of "come on, boys," he would go rushing down the field, kicking a ball or throwing one of us to the ground. On one occasion, he dragged me across the field not knowing that my back was badly sunburnt, and I can still remember the skin on my back peeling off like a snake shedding its skin. At night, all the caravan occupants went to the open-air club with its dancefloor. The kids would sit with their bottle of lemonade and packet of crisps while the adults chatted and drunk. Life was so much simpler then and I know it's debatable but the summers really did seem longer and with more sunshine.

My first school, St John's, was only yards away from Winterbourne House, and, being born in August, I had to start attendance at just over four years old rather than five as was the case then. My mother recalls that she had to take me on the first day screaming and kicking. At the end of the day, I informed my mum that it wasn't too bad but I didn't want to go there again. It must have come as a huge shock to learn the truth. In those days, Winterbourne House was like a vertical village where you knew most of the neighbours and went to school with their kids. There wasn't a great turnover of the flats with most of the families staying for life and then the grown-up children taking over the rent. I recall that there were quite a lot of inter-family marriages and you always knew when someone had died because there would be someone collecting for a wreath. Once a year, many families from the road made the move to Kent for the hop picking. One morning an open flatbed lorry would arrive, and couches, mattresses, and everything needed for life in the fields were loaded up with the wives and children piling on top, and the exodus began. I always envied these kids as it all sounded great fun but I was never allowed to go as my parents thought that there were lots of "goings-on" in the evenings, but that only intrigued me even more.

As a child, I suffered all the childhood illnesses which in those days were just the norm: German measles, whooping cough, chicken pox, mumps, etc. If you could get it, I did. The illness that really set me back in the early years was asthma and the two accompanying conditions, eczema and hay fever. I seem to recall that the only medications dished out by your local GP (at a shilling a visit before the blessed NHS came to be) were phenobarbitone and calamine lotion, and both didn't do much good. When I started to become short-sighted at about seven I was prescribed NHS glasses but anyone from that time knows they were horrible wire things and I had to have the ear pieces taped up due to my allergy to metal—did I mention that was another problem of my childhood? One good thing to come out of my metal allergy was that after a couple of years suffering from scabby ears and humiliation at the hands of my schoolmates, the doctor finally authorised plastic frames on the wonderful NHS and I was told by the optician that I was the very first schoolboy in London to be given these lovely all-plastic frames free of charge. I suffered this condition until I was fifteen, when it just disappeared, but during those years my dear parents tried every weird cure they read about. Inhaling bowls of strange herbs and leaves, frozen cold baths first thing in the morning, and, weirdest of all, bear fat, which they sent for from Canada, rubbed into my chest every night. I certainly didn't have a sickly childhood and given some of the illnesses about in those days, polio being the big one, I think myself lucky that my medical problems were only minor.

One regular visitor to Portland Road was the rag-and-bone man who, like *Steptoe and Son*, usually came on his horse and cart. You could take a few old clothes or something metal and exchange it for a goldfish in an old jam jar. I remember doing this on a couple of occasions and both times the fish died after a few days. The better option was to take those clothes, or a large bundle of newspapers, to the rag shop in Warmer Road and get money for the items instead of some half-dead aquatic life form. What a completely different world Portland Road was in those days—bombed out buildings and a corner shop selling coal. Some of the old buildings could probably have been bought for next to nothing and now they're worth millions. Oh, to have had hindsight!

*My sister Pat and I.*

\*\*\*

# Chapter 2

## *Dirty Granddads*

I have always told people that I had the dirtiest grandparents one could possibly have, one being a miner the other being a chimney sweep. My paternal grandparents were William and Susan Howe, née Morse, and my maternal grandparents were Margaret Harding, née Kettle, and Sidney Proudfoot. William, or Bill as he was called, had a small chimney sweeping business. His family consisted of six boys and seven girls; they had a further three children who had died. Although the boys were all made to work for their father at one time or other, I don't think that any were required to climb up the chimneys. Records show that my grandparents got married at All Saints Church, Notting Hill, on 25 December 1897 when William was twenty years old and Susan was eighteen.

Before I was born, the Howe family lived at 18 Uxbridge Street in Notting Hill Gate. My father once told me that he had the chance to buy the house but, hating debt, he declined. Last year a house in that street sold for £2,495,000. C'est la vie. The house was brought by Ben and Bebe Daniels from the well-known radio programme *Life with the Lyons*. The show, which also featured their real-life son, Richard, and daughter, Barbara, ran on BBC and independent television from 1954 until 1960.

By the time I was around, the Howe family had moved to Lime Grove in Shepherd's Bush, famous of course for one of the first BBC television studios.

My sister Pat tells me that it was her responsibility to take me to Lime Grove to see my grandparents and that we both hated the visit as apparently my grandfather was the grumpiest man in the family. Lime Grove has more happy memories for both Pat and I as we both swam in galas and competitions at the baths there. In fact, at one all-London schoolboy contest I came second in the freestyle event, my greatest sporting achievement.

My maternal grandparents had a family of four girls and one boy. My grandmother's first husband was a Mr Golightly who was gassed in the First World War and later died. Mr Proudfoot, her second husband and father of my mother, was a miner and worked in the Seghill mine and, like a large number of miners at the time, he later died of pneumoconiosis, more commonly referred to as "black lung disease" or just "black lung" and caused by exposure to coal dust.

With all these aunts and uncles, I had a great many cousins of my own age. Unfortunately, most of them moved out of the London area in the Fifties. The ones we saw a lot of were my aunt Dot and uncle Arthur's daughters, Ann and Susan, and my uncle Ernie and aunt Dorothy's daughters, Carol and Lorraine. Both sets of cousins were of the same age as my brother Peter and myself, and I readily admit to having a big crush on Carol. My uncle Ernie was a postman and the family lived, I think, in Pembroke Gardens, Kensington, where my aunt Dot was the housekeeper for a famous painter called Leonard Boden. Boden's daughter, Daphne, was the same age as my cousin Carol, so they became friends and my affections moved from one to the other, but alas were never noticed or acted upon. When, as a family, we visited my uncle Ernie, we were sometimes given a sneaky peek into the studio at the back of the house to marvel at the half-finished portrait of some famous person, and on the rare occasion were told that the famous person was present in the studio.

Leonard Monroe Boden was a British portrait painter born in Greenock in Renfrewshire, Scotland, in 1911. It was in Glasgow that he met his wife, Margaret Tulloch, and they married in 1937. Boden and his wife later studied at Heatherley School of Fine Art in London and worked together on illustrating books in the 1930s. Their daughter, Daphne, became a harpist and was the first British harpist to be awarded the Premier Prix for Harp at the Brussels Royal Conservatoire. She also became a professor of harp at the Royal College of Music and the Royal Academy of Music. Following the war, Boden began to paint portraits, gaining a reputation for his depictions of actors such as Alastair Sim and Donald Wolfit, and the singer Boris Christoff. A portrait of Field Marshal Lord Milne was Boden's first large-scale commission in 1954. Future portraits of notable dignitaries included three Lord Mayors of London and Margaret Thatcher. Pope Pius XII was painted by Boden in 1957; it was the only portrait that Pius granted sittings for and the portrait hung in the Pontiff's summer residence in Castelgandolfo and later moved to the Vatican. Margaret, Boden's wife, would often contribute to his portraits, with their efforts having been described as "a joint operation".

My lovely uncle called Arthur, who had served in the Merchant Navy during the war and had seen most of the world, was a fascinating character. He had brought back from China a silver opium pipe which I really coveted but don't think I know what it was for. During his Navy days, he had learned to be a barber to the crew and once a month, lured by my mother's cooking, he came to our new flat in Winterbourne House to cut my dad's, my brother's, and my hair. This was not a wonderful evening for me as at the time I was hoping to look like Tony Curtis and ended up looking like one of the Three Stooges, and if you don't know what they looked like, think pudding basins!

In London, we saw very little of my Northumberland relatives except when Newcastle were playing in the FA Cup Final, and then my mother's brother Fred and an adopted cousin Ralph descended on us for a meal, but they never seemed to stay the night. My uncle Fred was an accountant who worked for a large tobacco company in Newcastle. He also did the books of a Chinese restaurant and before he retired was looking after the financial affairs of several Chinese restaurants; needless to say, Fred liked his food and the restaurants fed him very well. Uncle Fred and Aunty Vi had a son, Trevor, who was born with Down's Syndrome and only lived until his thirties. He was a big and happy lad and my mother was in the habit, when visiting her brother, of taking Trevor for a walk. On one such walk, Trevor, who was about twice the size of Mum, decided he wanted to go to the toilet and with the cry of "come on, Auntie Carrie, I need a wee!" half dragged my poor mum into the gent's public toilet which, much to my mother's relief, was empty at the time. Trevor liked going out in the family car, a big old Rover, but always wanted to drive, so Uncle Fred had a false steering wheel fitted to the passenger side. Bearing in mind that Trevor was almost the size of his father, I could only imagine the looks of disbelief on the faces of Newcastle drivers as they went past.

One of my mother's sisters we saw a lot of was my aunt Peg who was married to a policeman named Robert Todd who hailed from Edinburgh and was known to us kids as Uncle Jock. My memories of Aunt Peg and Uncle Jock go back to 1953 and the coronation of Queen Elizabeth. Jock was a warrant officer stationed at Northwood where he lived in the flat above the police station and was the only one we knew with a television. So, on that memorable day in June, we travelled to Northwood to watch this spectacular event on Aunt Peg's nine-inch-screen TV. Looking back, I think Jock was a bit of a sadist as during another visit to Northwood he gave my brother Peter and I a tour of the station and cells; urging us to view the cell from the inside, he promptly shut the door and turned the lights off. I was far from happy but poor Peter, who was only six, was terrified and we were not released for a good ten minutes and were then given a lecture on what would happen if we strayed from the path of law and order.

*Granddad Bill with some of the family.*

*Maternal grandparents with my mother, the smallest of her sisters, and her brother Fred.*

\*\*\*

# Chapter 3

## *Dad's War*

When Dad was called up to join the war effort he was enlisted in the Royal Artillery and at first saw more of Crewe station rather than any fighting, that being the main station to change trains en route to various army camps. He went on to serve in North Africa but mainly served in Italy and was awarded the 1939–45 Star, Africa Star, Italy Star, The Defence Medal, and The War Medal. All Dad's medals and some photographs are now on display at the Eden Camp Museum, Yorkshire, located on the outskirts of the market town of Melton in North Yorkshire. Eden Camp is a modern history theme museum housed within the grounds of an original World War II prisoner-of-war camp. First opened to the public in 1987, it has since grown into one of the largest and most comprehensive museums covering British military history.

During the latter part of the conflict, Dad found himself serving in an Italian prisoner-of-war camp and tells of a scam that was going on between one member of his company and a member of the British Military Police. The artillery man would sell or exchange a used pair of army boots to one of the released Italian soldiers and his mate in the military police would stop him down the road and confiscate the boots as being stolen army property. Dad claimed that the same pair of boots was sold more than fifty times. This of course could have been just an old Tommy's tale, rather like the Italian tanks he used to talk about that had one forward and four reverse gears. Dad spent the last days of the war in Naples as a Staff Sergeant and by all accounts enjoyed his time there. When he died, we found a photograph in his papers of a small female child with an inscription on the back in Italian. We of course had the same thoughts as anyone reading this, but the inscription turned out to be just a thank you for some small gifts; however, I still can't help thinking that somewhere along the Italian coast is someone who looks a lot like my sister!

My father was a very talented man and for someone who left school at fourteen, his handwriting and grammar were A Level standard. He was also a very good artist, specialising in watercolours but using any sort of paint he could get his hands on. He painted many a small landscape, usually copying a postcard or a page out of a magazine. I remember my bedroom at Winterbourne House was decorated with Dad's hand-painted Disney cartoon characters that would have put some of today's illustrators to shame. When I got older these lovey paintings were covered up with wallpaper and I have often been tempted when I'm in London to call in at the flat and see if they are still there under layers of wallpaper. My grandfather stopped Dad taking up a scholarship at the Graycoats School in London, and I wonder how far he would have got with further education?

In 1946, a big event, although I didn't think it was that great at the time, to happen that year was the birth of my brother Peter. My father, having spent the past six years in the army, I suppose, was used to doing everything by numbers and in order and that is the only explanation I can think of as to why Peter was born on 11 August, my birthday. I can just about recall my sister Pat coming into my bedroom and telling me I had a baby brother for my birthday. This was a huge disappointment to me as I was

16

expecting a bike. Shortly after this monumental event, and because I was born in August, I was required to start school rather earlier than most of the kids in the area. St John's School could not have been more convenient to attend, being at the back of Winterbourne House, a matter of a few yards. I was taken on the first day, kicking and screaming, by my mother, but after that had to go by myself and it came as a big shock that I was expected to go five days a week.

Winterbourne House was like a small four-storey village. We knew most of the families living there—the Rawlings, the Dummits, the Armstrongs, who lived next door, the Chamberlains, the Hillyards, and many more. A lot of the kids from these families were of the same age as myself so of course went to the same school. I did fairly well at a primary school level, coming in the top five in most subjects, but I still failed the 11-plus exam. One of the few teachers I remember, and the one who helped and encouraged me, was Mr Scott. Mr Scott was an ex-military man who had a false leg and a fearsome manner; he was the only one who the pupils were scared of and kept a strict discipline in his class, but I owe a lot to that man as he persuaded me at age twelve to sit the examination for entry to a technical college. A friend and fellow pupil at the school who later captained the England football team was Alan Mullery. After enjoying a successful career with Fulham and Tottenham Hotspur in the 1960s and 1970s, he became a manager working with several different clubs. He is also famous for being the first ever England player to be sent off in an international match.

My father was a great dad; he spent a lot of time taking my brother and I out to places of interest in London. It was through Dad that I got to know the museums and buildings of London. One of his and our favourite places to go was the

Natural History Museum in South Kensington, but it wasn't the dinosaurs or the life-size model of the blue whale that we came to see, it was a stuffed greyhound! I should point out that one of my father's vices was gambling, and in particular greyhound racing. Dad always used to say that the greyhound we were marched to see, "Mick the Miller", had won him quite a few pounds and he was just paying his respects. Mick the Miller was a male brindle greyhound whose achievements included winning nineteen races in a row. Mick died on 6 May 1939, a few weeks short of his thirteenth birthday. After his death he was stuffed and given by his owner to the Natural History Museum. He has since been moved to the Natural History Museum at Tring in Hertfordshire where he is still on public view.

Dad loved his gambling but never went beyond a certain level. His main love was horse racing, followed by greyhound racing, and, in later life, bingo. Most Saturday afternoons Dad could be found in front of the television with a Sporting Life in one hand and his betting slips in the other. He would never tell my mother which horses he had bet on but on very rare occasions, mostly on the big events, like the Derby and Grand National, she wheedled it out of him and when his horses came nowhere he would blame Mum for "putting the mockers on the race". When Dad retired he and Mum moved back to Northumberland and that's when his bingo period started. Dad was always a great walker and going to a bingo hall from his house in Seaton Delaval he had to walk to Whitley Bay, quite some distance. Dear old Dad never had many wins, but Mum knew when he had won a few pounds because a box of her favourite chocolates (chocolate gingers) would appear on the sideboard. I joke that when he died on 3 June 1986, aged eighty, he left me a battered old briefcase containing a chest full of medals and some old betting slips, but I wouldn't have wanted it any other way. Dad passed away as most of us would like to go. My mother was getting breakfast when she heard a crash and, when she went into the bedroom to see what had caused it, found my dad on the floor, dead. He had probably not been to see a doctor for about twenty years but ten days before he died my mother persuaded him to see their GP to get something for a touch of flu. The doctor gave him a thorough examination and this visit to the doctor was enough to save him, and us, the trauma of a post mortem. In gambling my father was never very lucky but in life he really was a winner. After Dad died Mum was very lonely and despite having some good friends and visits from myself, she missed Dad to the point that she confessed she was ready to go the way of her lovely husband, and after a short illness she died peacefully on 19 March 1987, aged seventy-eight, in North Shields Hospital. Both my parents passed away without any trouble to their children. I had been at my mother's bedside—by this time she was unconscious—all day when a nurse persuaded me to pop home for a shower and a bite to eat, and when I returned to the hospital an hour and a half later she had peacefully passed away. She even spared me the trauma of seeing her go. I was so very lucky to have such wonderful parents.

\*\*\*

# Chapter 4

## *Notting Hill Life*

Living in Portland Road was comparatively upmarket to some of the surrounding areas and when I read Alan Johnson's wonderful book *This Boy* I realise just how lucky we were. The former Home Secretary's memories of his extreme childhood poverty in Southall Street was a real eye-opener, an inspiration to me, and encouraged me to put pen to paper relating my own experiences growing up in that part of West London. In so many ways, Alan Johnson, who I have always thought was one of the best politicians in today's Britain (no, I am not a Labour supporter) and I have a mirrored upbringing but without the poverty and degradation. Although older than Mr Johnson, we seemed to have lived a parallel existence. I went to the same Saturday morning pictures at the Electric Cinema (Bug Hole) in Portobello Road, swam at the same baths, and so many other shared childhood and teenage experiences in the Notting Hill area. My father in later life was a postman at the Westbourne Grove sorting office and as a student I myself worked at that sorting office over one Christmas. I also served as a civil servant in the Home Office and he has been Home Secretary, and, needless to say, we are also lifelong QPR supporters.

House of Commons
Westminster
LONDON
SW1A 0AA
6th October 2014

Dear Mr Howe,

My apologies for this disgracefully late reply to the letter you sent me in January.

My only excuse is that I have indeed been writing "a further episode" and it's taken every spare minute.

We do have a lot in common. I know Portland Rd very well and I knew that Alan Mullery was a local boy (who eventually came to play for and manage the Superhoops as I recall).

I hope you're enjoying retirement in Cheshire and thank you so much for your kind words about the book (and for being one of the small army of dedicated followers of This Week). Once again profuse apologies for this late response.

Best wishes
Alan Johnson

21

A must for all kids in the Notting Hill area was the Electric Cinema on Saturday mornings. Designed by architect Gerald Seymour Valentin in the Edwardian Baroque style, it originally opened as the Electric Cinema Theatre. During World War I, an angry mob attacked the Electric, believing that its German-born manager was signalling to Zeppelin raiders from the roof, after nearby Arundel Gardens was hit by a bomb dropped from a Zeppelin. Later, in 1932, the Electric became the Imperial Playhouse cinema, though by this time the Portobello Road area had become rather run down, along with the rest of Notting Hill. In the late 1960s it changed its name again, becoming the Electric Cinema Club, showing mostly independent and Avant Garde movies. At the Imperial Playhouse, or the Bug Hole as us kids called it, the seats in the 1950s for the Saturday morning pictures came in two prices—threepence and sixpence old money. The three penny seats in the front were wooden with no padding but the six penny ones at the back were covered in a lovely red cloth. Kids, and I'm ashamed to say myself included, were in the habit of paying our threepence and, when the lights went down, sneaking to the posher seats at the back. This practice had its drawbacks as if you were discovered you were thrown out and missed that week's episode of *Roy Rogers* and *Flash Gordon*. On one occasion, I successfully made the move but paid the price as after the performance, and of course wearing short trousers at the time, my legs were covered in flea bites. I think that kept me on the straight and narrow from then on. It was in this cinema that I had my first cigarette, which was almost my last as I hated it and felt quite ill.

During the late 1940s, the notorious mass murderer John Christie was thought to have worked at the Electric as a projectionist. Christie was a notorious English serial killer active during the 1940s and early 1950s. He murdered at least eight women, including his wife Ethel, at 10 Rillington Place, Notting Hill, London. Two of Christie's victims were Beryl Evans and her daughter, Geraldine. Beryl's husband, Timothy, was tried and hanged in 1950 for the murder of his wife and daughter, but three years later, Christie's crimes were discovered and it is now accepted that it was Christie who had committed the murders. Christie was arrested and convicted of his wife's murder, for which he was hanged. Rillington Place being quite near to Portland Road, and with Christie on the run at the time, it was only natural for schoolboys of my age to want to see where the grisly deeds had been carried out. With two of my friends, I walked up to Rillington Place to find a little crowd gathered around the front garden of the house where an enterprising young man, still known in the Fifties as a "spiv", had knocked down the small garden wall and was attempting to sell the bricks for a shilling each. The fascinating and brilliant film *10 Rillington Place* with Richard Attenborough is an almost-documentary of events of the time.

As well as the streets around Portland Road, my playgrounds also took in Holland Park, Kensington Gardens, and Hyde Park. A favourite in the summer months was to go swimming in the Serpentine Lido, but our entry to the lido was not through the fee-paying turnstile but via the lake upstream. To this end, the famous Peter Pan statue played a major part. We would go behind the statue and leave our clothes in the bushes, enter the lake just in front of Peter Pan, and swim the short distance to the lido where we could mingle with the fee-paying patrons. We were never caught and I think our only concern was that another gang of kids would find our clothes and hide them somewhere else. It's a long way to walk back to Portland Road in wet swimming trunks! Peter Pan in Kensington Gardens is a bronze statue by sculptor Sir George Frampton, installed in 1912. The sculpture was commissioned by the author J.M. Barrie and based on the literary character first published in 1902.

Portland Road was a totally different place in the Forties, Fifties, and Sixties from what it is today. I think the first sign of an upmarket trend in the road was the opening of Julie's Restaurant in 1969 in what was originally a builder's yard. Julie's is named after interior designer Julie Hodgess who conceived both Julie's Restaurant and Bar. It has been a magnet for over forty years from the hippie generation to the ultra-cool London set of today and when it opened my father said, "I'll give it six months, it won't last." Dad, it's still doing very well. When my brother Peter came over from the USA with his wife a few years ago, we took a trip down memory lane and had dinner at Julie's for the first time. It was probably the first time either of us could have afforded it.

I can't think for the life of me now why, when as a 13-year-old and wanting to join the Scouts, I chose a troop in Marylebone. It could have been that I knew somebody already in the troop but the reason escapes me. Suffice to say I spent hours travelling from Holland Park tube station to Edgware Road each Friday evening as the troop met in the basement of the big church just along from the tube station. The Scout Master's name was Mr Weller and he was, as I recall, a lovely kind man. He was a Harry Secombe lookalike and strangely enough could sing almost as well as the great goon. Over time, I rose through the scouting ranks to become a Patrol Leader and went on several counties and one international Jamboree. I also swam for the

Marylebone district, winning a couple of trophies, which I rank as one of my greatest achievements—sad, isn't it? Mr Weller had the added attraction for us 13- to 14-year-olds: he travelled on a Matchless motorbike with a sidecar. He had a daughter about our age but she was no match for that great bike, and unfortunately, she was the spitting image of her father so didn't enter into the equation. At times when we paraded on a Saturday, or after the church parade on Sunday, Mr Weller took three of us, with tremendous arguments as to who rode on the pillion and who had to settle for the sidecar, to his home for tea. In today's seemingly endless reports in the media of sexual assaults on young people it seems incredible that our parents allowed these trips, but they had all met Mr Weller and he was a genuinely nice man, and I have nothing but good memories of my scouting years.

My dad and I had always been keen boxing fans; some of my pocket money every month went on *The Ring* magazine, which I read from cover to cover. At about fourteen years of age I thought I would get some boxing training and join a club, and the nearest place was the not-very-aptly named Rugby Club in Warmer Road. I never did find out why it was called the Rugby Club as no rugby was ever played there. Luckily, one of the trainers at the club, Mr Wilson, lived along the same balcony as ourselves and took me along one evening. I loved the training, the skipping, the medicine ball, and the shadow boxing, etc., but a big problem for me was my height and weight. At fourteen years I was already five feet ten inches and weighed some nine and a half stone, so was always matched for sparring with lads who were sixteen plus. As you can imagine, I tended to take a lot more punishment than I gave and after many months and having my nose reshaped, I suspended my ambitions in the ring for the next year. However, you can't keep a stupid man down and within a few months I was persuaded to return to the ring by the opening of a boxing section to another boy's club in the area, the Quest Club at 85 Clarendon Road. The boxing was run by a local police officer who I remember being called Bing. He had the distinction of being the first Metropolitan Police Officer in modern times to be allowed to grow a full beard. Also coaching the boys was a small Indian guy who we called Robin and who was rumoured to be a flyweight champion in India. Of course, I was faced with the same problem as at the Rugby Club but loved the training, so endured the occasional black eye, and Bing was more aware of health and safety, so I took less punishment. It is nice to see that the Quest is still there but now is a day centre for the elderly.

I remember our home life and entertainment centred around the wireless, with the highlight of my week being *Dick Barton: Special Agent.* Our wireless (radio to any younger readers) was rented from a company called Radio Rentals. It was fed by cable and had very few stations, but one you could tune into was Radio Luxenberg, which my father literally hated but I loved. Dad disliked loud music of all sorts and I was banned from listening to Luxenberg when he was home. The problem was solved when for one of my birthdays I was given a Crystal Radio/Cat's Whisker set to make your own wireless and a pair of earphones. There was an enormous variety of Crystals sets or Cat's Whisker radios that were manufactured for the domestic market and were sold as complete radios, but there was also a booming market in kits and the components and many people made their own radios at home. My kit came with all the components but without the box to house them. Dad put this right by making me a small plywood box and helped me put it all together. I couldn't describe the sound quality as recording studio but at least I was able to listen to the rock stars of the day without the magic shout: "Turn that rubbish off."

In the early Fifties, a craze that seemed to take over my family was rag rug making. Being Dad and his army training, this wasn't just a one-off item but an organised production line. He made a large wooden frame which canvas was stretched over, and sent for a pair of implements to push small strips of material through the canvas. Dad's job was to draw the patterns on the canvas. Mum used a cut-throat razor to cut the one inch by two inch strips, and Peter and I followed the pattern and pushed the cloth through. Pete and I thought it hilarious that we were walking on one of Dad's old jackets, but those old rugs lasted forever and looked okay.

\*\*\*

# Chapter 5

## *Mum and Dad*

*Robert Howe 26/5/1906*
*Caroline Howe, née Proudfoot, 12/7/1908*

*My handsome father and wonderful mother.*

When my father left school at fourteen, his first job was at the Coronet Cinema in Notting Hill Gate, showing people to their seats, operating the safety curtains, and as a general dogsbody. He later went to work at the department store Barkers in Kensington High Street as a delivery van boy where he progressed to a driver and stayed there until he was called up for the Army.

The Coronet was designed as a theatre by leading architect W. G. R. Sprague at a cost of £25,000, and opened in 1898. Famous actors who appeared at the theatre in its early days included Sarah Bernhard, and in 1916, films were shown at the theatre for the first time as part of variety programmes mixing live and filmed performances. In 1923, it became a cinema full-time and capacity was reduced from 1,143 to 1,010 seats but it retained, as it still does, its original theatre interior. In 1950, it was renamed the Gaumont and the upper tier was closed for seating, and in 1972, the Rank Organisation (which had taken over Gaumont) proposed to demolish the building, but a local campaign based upon its architectural merit and its interesting history secured its survival and, indeed, refurbishment. In 1977, it was sold by Rank to an independent cinema operator and its name reverted to the Coronet. In June 2014, it was acquired by a new owner with plans to turn the old place into a luxury cinema venue.

While working as a driver, Dad made frequent deliveries to Kensington Palace Gardens, which was nicknamed "Millionaires Row" due to the enormous houses and private road status. At that time, my mother had come to London at sixteen to work for a wealthy family called Proctor as an under-nanny to her older sister, my aunt Peg. My father was a handsome man in his twenties and although Mum was seeing a policeman at the time, she decided that Dad was the better bet and they married on 21 April 1930. My parents had four children, the first of which, Irene, was born premature in 1931 but died after only a few days. Next came Patricia Margaret, born on 23 February 1932, then me born 11 August 1942, and lastly Peter, born 11 August 1946.

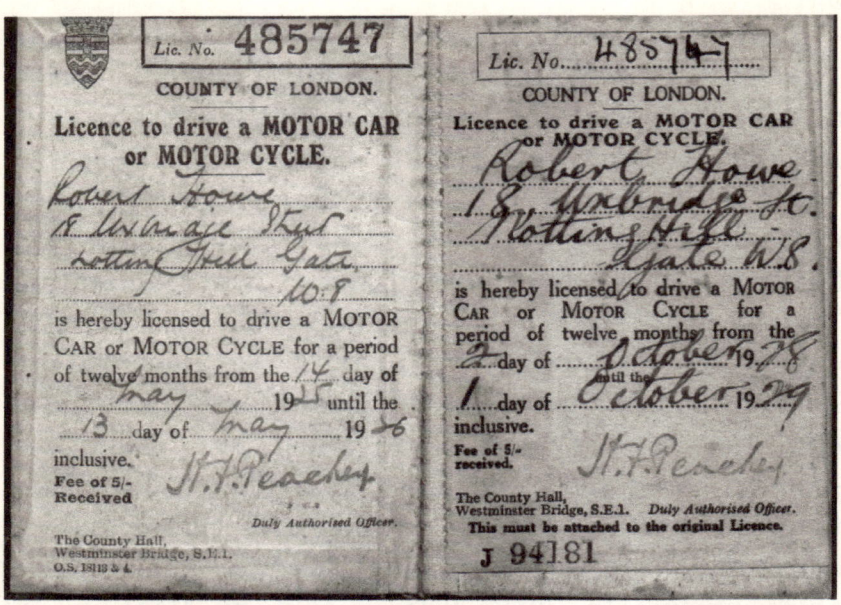

*Dad's first driving licence, dated 14 May 1925.*

My mother Caroline, having worked as a cook during the war, was, as you would expect, a wonderful cook, and I very much regret not having paid the attention her meals deserved. She baked the most amazing cakes but I would always prefer a shop-bought one. It was only after I left home that I began to really appreciate Mum's cooking and, of course, her Sunday dinners have never been equalled; however, my sister Pat came quite close. Mum always seemed to be in the kitchen and in her last few years moved into sweets and chocolate making. Whenever my wife and I paid a visit home there was always a box of homemade chocolate gingers to take away with us and, being Linda's favourite, that was always greatly appreciated. By today's standards, Mum's cooking was quite simple, but her baked Alaska would not have been out of place in any five-star restaurant today.

With an age gap of ten years, my sister Pat had to take some of the responsibility in bringing me up, which couldn't have been that easy for her as a ten-year-old and later as a teenager. I can remember two of her boyfriends: a guardsman, who gave me a webbing belt with all the Guards regiment badges attached, and Michael Hersey, her future husband. Mike, who was called George in the early years, was doing his National Service when Pat met him, serving in the RAF Military Police. After their first son, Richard, was born on 18 March 1954, the family emigrated to South Africa in August 1957, where Mike's family had moved many years before. A daughter, Susan, was born on 14 August 1959, but it was many years before we saw them all again.

I remember when Richard was born. I was twelve and Pete was eight. We were given a two-shilling coin to give to the new baby by Mum, and off we set to walk from Portland

Road to Notting Hill where my sister lived. This particular day happened to be Mother's Day and we hadn't got my mother any flowers, etc. I had a brainwave and we changed the one two-shilling coin for two one-shilling coins; problem solved when we put one shilling into Richard's hand and on the way home bought Mum a nice bunch of daffodils. Where would I be now if I had carried that streak of initiative over to the rest of my adult life?

My brother Peter at one time seemed to follow me into everything, first the same school, Christopher Wren, and later a short spell in the Merchant Navy, but after that our lives couldn't have been more different. Peter was always interested in animals and got himself a job at the London Zoo as a keeper. His behind the scenes tours of the various animal houses he looked after were something to behold. The reptile house where they kept a nasty alligator living behind the exhibits corridor because it was too aggressive to be put with the others, the small breeding rooms where the zoo bred thousands of flies and insects to feed the other reptiles and hundreds of mice for the same purpose. Looking down on a bunch of rattlesnakes from the platform behind the tanks was an experience not many were able to do. I have fed rhinos and had the biggest python in the zoo draped around my shoulders, and will never forget Pete's private tours. While working in the snake house, Peter, who was still living at home, had the opportunity to bring home a small royal python to look after. My father wasn't entirely happy, and especially so when he learnt that the snake was one who would not eat dead pray and would need to be fed two live mice every week. This arrangement went well until my brother announced that the snake was getting rather big and that he would need to feed it small rabbits instead of mice! The answer from Dad was "That goes or you do," and knowing the expense of living away from home, the snake went back to the zoo.

When Peter left the Merchant Navy, he and I spent a lot time with an old shipmate of mine, Gwyn Harding, probably the biggest character I have ever met in a lifetime of knowing great characters. Peter and Gwyn, who were out of work at the time, decided to go into business together and came up with a scheme to set up a mobile canteen on various building sites in the area. The pair rented an old, rather isolated house in Buckinghamshire where they moved in with Gwyn's girlfriend and set about feeding building workers and road repairers. The next time I saw my little brother some weeks later he was driving a Jaguar car and Gwyn had a Daimler Dart sports car. I later learnt that Gwyn had done a bit of dealing in second-hand cars and both ventures were doing very nicely, however the partnership didn't last very long and sadly I lost contact with this mad Welshman. One of my biggest regrets in life was that I turned down an offer to buy the Daimler Dart when Gwyn asked if I wanted to buy it at a very good price. We had some great times, the three of us. The family of Gwyn's girlfriend, Romaine, had a small farm in Stoke Poges, Slough, where we spent most Sundays; and at the local hostelry, The One Pin, with Sunday lunch at the farm. After one mammoth lunch, Romaine's mother said that Peter and I could have a chicken to take home, but failed to tell us that it was still running around the farmyard. As city boys, we had no idea how to despatch the poor bird, and after several attempts to catch it we decided that we would in fact prefer fish and chips for our Sunday dinner, and the bird was spared for another day.

I once went on a pub crawl with Gwyn around the Earls Court area, finishing at the Windsor Castle in Notting Hill

Gate. I think we visited some twelve pubs and Gwyn had a pint in every one while I stuck to half pints, and at the end of the evening I was seeing double while Gwyn seemed stone cold sober. He insisted on driving back to his flat in Earls Court and at a set of lights on Cromwell Road he failed to stop and gently went into the car in front which had stopped on the red light. Like a flash, Gwyn got out of the car and began to remonstrate with the driver in front for backing into his car. The driver was so shocked that Gwyn was able, after telling the poor driver that he didn't intend to claim on the man's insurance on this occasion, to get back in his car and drive around the innocent driver who just sat there.

On one of our nights out, Gwyn introduced me to a real experience in the form of Schmidt's German restaurant in Charlotte Street, near Oxford Street. The elderly German waiters were all self-employed and were surly to the point of rudeness (except to German or Austrian expats of their own generation), but they did provide silver service (when the food eventually arrived). The waiting times were unbelievable but the food was cheap and usually good.

Frederick Schmidt was an immigrant butcher from Wurtenberg who became a British citizen and served during the First World War as an army cook. He opened Schmidt's on his return from the war. Apparently, the Soviet spy Donald Maclean spent his last day in Britain at the restaurant before fleeing to the Soviet Union in May 1951. Schmidt's closed down after a few generations existence; it opened in 1901, closing in the late Seventies.

My brother Peter's love of looking after animals changed somewhat in his next job, which was a full-time whipper-in at the Tynedale Fox Hunt. He recalls that the huntsman who he worked under was a real hard task master, but he soon learned to ride, and his love of hunting and country sports is still strong to this day. In the years before his retirement he became huntsman at the Newcastle and District Beagles, The London Hunt Club in Canada, and the Red Mountain Hunt in North Carolina. He still lives in North Carolina but having come off his horse numerous times and broken various bones, at seventy, he no longer hunts on horseback but still follows his local hunt on a quad bike while his lovely wife Suzanne rides to hounds.

Having Peter in the family with his hunting pedigree, it was almost inevitable that I would take an interest in hunting, but not being able to afford the fees and horse hire needed for fox hunting, I went for a Beagle pack that hunt on foot. I had been out with Peter when he was huntsman at the Newcastle and District Beagles so knew the form, and with his introduction I was readily accepted into the Cheshire Beagle Hunt. After a couple of years, I was asked to become a member and was duly elected as such, remaining a member for a further eight years. I was always more interested in the social side of hunting, although following hounds (never dogs) on foot is a great way to keep fit, the hunt teas and dinners are usually tremendous, and the characters you meet are unforgettable. A real character who came out with the Cheshire Beagles on one occasion was Clarissa Wright-Dickson, the sadly departed celebrity chef and television personality. Miss Wright-Dickson was never known for her dress sense or indeed her style of dressing, but seen out in the hunting field she would have embarrassed a scruffy bag lady. She was such a strong character that she would have not given a fig to what anyone else thought about her clothes, and good on her for that. A few years after meeting her out with the Beagles, I spoke to her at a food festival held in Nantwich, Cheshire, where she was promoting her latest cookery book. Still dressed the same and with the same directness of manner, we talked for a few moments about her book which I regret to say I forgot to buy and missed the opportunity to have a signed copy. She sadly passed away in 2014 and this country was left without one of the most interesting woman of her time. She had done it all.

Some years ago, I found that I was unable to keep up with the hounds (age and dodgy knees) and the prospect of just watching from a vantage point didn't really appeal, so sadly I resigned from the Cheshire Beagle Hunt. I still feel that to see a pack of hounds followed by the field of horses and riders crossing the Cheshire countryside is one of England's great sights.

When Parliament started debating hunting in 2002, the Countryside Alliance organised a protest march in London. Over 400,000 people from across the country marched through central London to highlight the needs of rural communities and to stop a ban on hunting. I took time off to join the march and it was a truly memorable day. Crowds were so big it took people queuing at the start of the official route more than six hours to filter through and was the biggest march ever held in this country. Hunting horns blared, whistles shrieked, and everyone had a great day. Remarkably, there was no trouble, except for a few hunt saboteurs trying to disrupt the day. For me, there were three highlights to my day. The first was seeing Boris Johnson marching a few feet from me pushing a pram containing one child while another held onto his hand. I very much regret not speaking to him as I will probably never get the opportunity again and he is something of a hero of mine after he introduced "Boris Bikes" to London. The next highlight happened in Pall Mall, the centre of gentleman's clubs. As we were marching along this road, a very distinguished looking gentleman dressed in country tweeds and plus fours left the marchers and rang the doorbell of the Reform Club. The door was opened by a butler in full morning suit who bowed to the gentleman who then turned to his fellow marchers and, to a huge cheer, gave a rather royal wave before entering the club for his lunch. The third highlight was my own lunch taken in a great little Italian restaurant in Soho. A very enjoyable day.

*Mum, Pete, and me—or is it the Kray twins?*

\*\*\*

# Chapter 6

## *Christopher Wren and me*

Christopher Wren started out as a building and art technical college at its old location in the Fox's School, Kensington Palace, between Kensington Church Street and Notting Hill Gate. The Fox School was originally founded as a charity school in 1842, and was my father's primary school. In the Eighties, Christopher Wren merged with Hammersmith County Girls School, and in 1990 it was renamed "The Phoenix High School".

Before the move to a new building in the Bloemfontein Road, Shepherd's Bush, the school used temporary premises at Latimar School in the Fulham Palace Road where I spent a year or so. In 1956, the new school opened with Mr Boot as our headmaster, and I spent the next few years happily achieving a poor academic education. Some of my fellow pupils who came after me achieved rather more prominence but seemingly none in the world of academia.

Paul Cook (1956–), English drummer, formerly of The Sex Pistols.

Steve Jones (1955–), English guitarist, formerly of The Sex Pistols.

Les Ferdinand (1966–), former England international footballer.

Dennis Wise (1966–), former England international footballer.

Jeff Chandler (1959–) former professional footballer.

Steve Parsons (1957–) former professional footballer.

George Lawrence (1962–), former professional footballer.

I had originally applied to enter the art department of Christopher Wren but at the interview, after the exam, I was told that my art submissions (hastily drawn the night before) didn't meet the requirements. I was offered a place in the building and architecture department and so my ambitions of becoming a second John Constable turned to becoming a second John Nash. My rejection from the art side of the college didn't mean that there were no art classes, but I was still feeling somewhat miffed, so along with a like-minded friend we decided to skip the art lesson and spend the afternoon at His Masters Voice record shop in Oxford Street. By not attending the first registration for that class we were not missed the whole term and spent many very happy afternoons in one of the booths at HMV listening to the sounds of the Fifties.

So, the time came when I reached sixteen and had to leave full-time education with no qualifications, little ambition, and not a clue what I wanted to do after I left.

I met some really good friends at Christopher Wrens and spent a large part of my teens and twenties in their company, but alas, over time we all seemed to go our separate ways and I have sadly lost touch with all of them. Ron Parissien, who left the building trade to become a Health Inspector at Smithfield Market, Dan Fryer, who moved to South Africa and started his own shop fitting business, Roy Watson went on to start a small heating and plumbing company, and Gerry Tench, last heard of in Australia. Together we all had some great times and frequented such venues as the Lyceum in the Strand, then a ballroom, the Hammersmith Palace, and at one time or another most of the coffee bars in Soho, favourites being the 2i's in Old Compton Street and the Macabre nearby. We had our first hamburger in one of the very first Wimpy Bars at the end of Old Compton Street.

The 2i's situated at 59 Old Compton Street was first run by two brothers, Freddie and Sammy Irani, hence the name of the café, "2i's Coffee Bar". Two Australian wrestlers, Paul "Dr Death" Lincoln and Ray "Rebel" Hunter, took over the lease and in September 1956, rock singer Tony Hicks was spotted by impresario John Kennedy, who was looking for someone or something that would set London's West End alight. Decca Records saw him, signed him up, and Hicks became the first British rock and roll star as "Tommy Steele". Just around the corner from the 2i's on Meard Street was Le Macabre, which used coffins as tables and Bakelite skulls for ashtrays. There were skull-shaped milk jugs, murals of skeletons and graveyards, and the jukebox featured the Funeral March.

As a group, rather than spend our limited resources having three or four pints in a pub, we tended to try and have one drink in some of the best hotels in central London, and by the age of eighteen I had been in some of the top London hotels. I admit that this wasn't the norm for teenagers in the late Fifties, but as a confidence builder it was first class, and of course we had to dress the part. Only Dan Fryer had a car but was happy to ferry the rest of us around and parking in London in those days wasn't the nightmare it is today, and as we only had the one drink and gallons of coffee, driving was also not a problem. One of the areas we liked was Mayfair and the colourful Shepherd's Market, well-known for its very friendly ladies of the night. Even if we had wanted to partake of the ladies' friendly offers, our pay scale wouldn't stretch to it, and so we had to be satisfied with just walking around and drinking coffee. It was on one of those walks back to the car that we passed a beautiful Aston Martin DB4. Dan said, "Have you seen my new car?" and proceeded to try the keys from his Morris Minor in the DB4. Wonder of wonders, they fitted, and the door opened. Of course, we had to see if the same key could turn the engine on and again, with a wonderful growl it fired up. I can't remember which one of us, Dan, Gerry, or myself, suggested it but we all seemed to think that a trip around the block and back wasn't out of the question. To cut a long story short, I had never been in the Hyde Park Underpass doing ninety miles an hour before. We, of course, never had any intention to keep the car and after half an hour or so we took it back to where it was parked. Unfortunately, the original space was now occupied, but luckily there was a vacant parking space some fifteen yards up from the original one and it was there that we left it without a scratch on it. We got some ten yards from where we had "borrowed" the car to find a very puzzled looking man scratching his head as he walked to his DB4.

Dan Fryer lived with this mother and an aunt, who were housekeepers to the Seligman family, in one of the best addresses in Holland Park, namely Illchester Place. Jonathan Miller, the British theatre and opera director, actor, and author, was a frequent visitor and I think may have been a relation. Dr Miller's documentary about the 1898 Torres Straits expedition, *Dr Miller and the Islanders*, certainly has a Seligman connection.

Gerry Tench haled from Fulham and lived with his parents and a younger sister who at a young age got into films. She played a child in the background in a couple of films, one of which was Tony Hancock's film *The Punch and Judy Man*. Gerry's mother, who chaperoned her daughter, used to tell us that off-camera, Hancock was the most miserable and ill-tempered man she had ever encountered. She also said that he hated kids.

Ron Parissien was a true Cockney who lived in Lambeth with his mother and younger sister. He was a very big lad and by the time he left school was well over six feet, but something of a gentle giant. Ron was the one who accompanied me on most visits to the Lyceum Ballroom. On those Friday nights out there was one thing you noticed about Ron—he was Elvis (Presley), always dressed the same, black loafers with red socks, black trousers, black shirt with a red tie, and a white jacket, and of course he had the sideboards. He thought he was the bee's knees, and indeed he was. It was during one of those nights that Ron met Janet. They later married and I was his best man. I went out for a short time with one of Janet's friends but this came to an end during a live television performance at the Lyceum for *The Six Five Special Show*. This was at the time of the hula hoop craze and I suffered the indignity of my friends seeing my girlfriend swinging a hula hoop around her neck rather than her waist.

I kept in touch with my old school friends but gradually, after I moved to Cheshire, we lost contact. One day I received a phone call from Gerry to tell me that he was following his elder brother and emigrating to Australia. He had sold his apartment in London and was planning to visit Thailand for a few weeks on his way to Australia and would I like to join him for a spell in Thailand—he would pay my fare. Offers like that don't come every day so I agreed. Had I known beforehand what the trip would be like I would have given a different answer. We set off from Heathrow by one of the worst airlines flying at the time, Tarom, the Romanian flag carrier which Gerry said had some remarkably cheap fares! The flight put down in the early hours of the morning in Bucharest and all the passengers were taken off and put into a very dark and cold holding lounge where our passports were taken by a gun-toting border guard. This is where I can claim to have worked for the Romanian Immigration Department. After about an hour, the border official returned and attempted to call out the passenger's names to return their passports. He was having such a struggle with the names I took my life in my hands, took the pile of passports from him, and quickly handed them back to their owners. We took off again shortly after. Before we landed at Bangkok, I had a terrible thought. Gerry had been known in the past to have partaken in the odd funny fag, and if he was stupid enough to be carrying a little something and I went through the controls with him—well, I like Hilton Hotels, but not the one in Bangkok where you all live in a large compound and I know what they do to good-looking white boys! I know my worries were unfounded but I was quite nervous walking from the plane. My worries disappeared when we reached the arrivals control and I spotted they had a channel for diplomats. This was at a time in the Eighties when I still travelled on a passport stamped with diplomatic status (see later chapter on Lagos). I barely had to show my passport and sailed through. The relief was immense, and of course, Gerry came through to landside half an hour after.

Our hotel for the first night was memorable as being the worst hotel I had ever stayed in by a factor of 100, booked of course by Gerry. It was like a concrete car park with rooms; there were stray dogs patrolling the corridors and the room had one faucet coming out of the wall over a cracked shower tray. I won't go into what the toilet was like, but arriving very early in the morning left me no choice; I had to stay the night. Although we were both jetlagged, Gerry decided to go to the bar next door for a night cap. I declined and tried to get what little sleep I could get in the room from hell. I didn't get much sleep, and by 7 a.m. Gerry had not returned. I uttered to myself a line from *Dad's Army,* "Don't panic, don't panic," and started to plan how I would get home and what to do with Gerry's clothes, when suddenly he came straggling in. He had fallen asleep in the bar and been gently mugged. Luckily, he had had the sense to leave most of his money and tickets in the room but was missing his watch. The holiday improved after the first night. I found a reasonable hotel and we did the sights of Bangkok before moving to Pattaya after a few days. By this time, Gerry had found female company and I was beginning to miss home, so I returned to Bangkok and changed my return ticket for the next day. If I thought the outward flight was eventful, the return one was equally interesting. I could be wrong but I'm pretty sure the following words don't exist in Romanian: "service", "friendliness", "smiling", "politeness", and "helpful", all terms or words totally unfamiliar to Tarom flight attendants. The flight to London is a long one but after seven hours there was no sign of any food or drink. When a passenger asked for a glass of water he was told "no water". Just as the braver passengers were on the point of hijacking the plane and flying it to the nearest airport with a McDonald's, food appeared. Not just one tray of food but two trays each, and each contained a complete three-course meal. However, the food was so bad that even one tray was too much/ I got a container of cherries in my tray that was passed its sell-by-date by, I would guess, three months, and they were rotten. We were all saved getting food poisoning when the plane nose-dived and went into the worst turbulence I have experienced which went on for the next four hours. I don't like Heathrow and always try to fly from a local airport but I was never so glad to land there in my life.

*Le Macabre had the distinction of being the only horror-themed café in London.*

\*\*\*

# Chapter 7

## *Violins—From Boy to Young Gentleman*

Due to leave school in 1958 without even the proverbial O Level in Woodwork, it was ironically the carpentry master, Mr Roberts, that I have to thank for my start in life. Mr Roberts, bless him, must have seen that I had some talent working with wood but was totally unsuitable for the rigours of the building site, and when he received an enquiry from W. H. Luff, a violin maker and restorer who had a workshop in nearby Wood Lane, to ask if the school had a suitable school leaver that he could take on and train, he kindly recommended me. I duly went along for an interview to the Wood Lane premises and got on splendidly with Mr Luff, who offered me the job at the princely salary of £1 & 10 shillings a week.

William H. Luff, violin maker: born in Essex, 7 September 1904; MBE, 1980; died in Worthing, Sussex, 30 November 1993. William Luff was one of the few great British violin makers of his time. His instruments are sought after and played by leading musicians all over the world. Luff was born into a musical family; his father was the well-known tenor Harry Luff and his uncle a violinist. He took lessons with a Russian who had studied with the legendary Leopold Auer in St Petersburg. He found a shop near the BBC TV Centre at Shepherd's Bush and decided not to open for a week so as to get the shop in order, but the news had spread and within a few hours a well-known teacher arrived carrying an armful of violins. From this moment business thrived, and during the years that followed many great violinists regularly crossed his threshold. One of Luff's most devoted customers was the late Albert Sammons. Luff also taught classes in violin making at the London College of Furniture, which today is part of the London Guildhall University.

I must have pleased Luff with my work and willingness to learn because after just two weeks he doubled my salary to £3 a week. Luff was a great teacher as well as being an extremely good boss; he would send me into Soho to pick up materials and varnishes from some of the incredible small stores there at the time, and at sixteen he arranged for me to open a bank account at his branch in Berners Street, which was an incredible thing for a boy of my age in the Fifties. I also got to meet well-known musicians and one time returned an instrument to the then-chairman of ICI, Paul Chambers. The shop was not the first place you would expect to meet young ladies, but there was a steady stream of music students passing through the shop and after a while, Luff encouraged me to serve them. It was while fitting a new string to her violin that I met and asked out a young American girl. On the appointed night, it was pouring with rain and Luff insisted on my taking his umbrella as in his words, "No gentleman should escort a young lady out without an umbrella". We went to the cinema in Leicester Square and afterwards walked down to Trafalgar Square where she asked me what the column was. I explained that it was Nelson and was shocked when she said, "Who's that?". There was no second date. It was William Luff who first showed me how wonderful classical music was and gave me a lifelong love of the genre. In fact, the first LP, as opposed to popular singles, I ever brought was Paganini's *Violin Concerto in D* and whenever I hear it being played I'm back in that varnish- and wood-smelling workshop in

W12. Luff insisted on calling me by my surname, and in front of his customers, Mr Howe. His logic was that when I reached middle and old age it would be very disrespectful for young musicians to call me by my Christian name. At this time, Luff ran an evening class in violin making at the London College of Furniture in Shoreditch. After I had been working for him for some time he asked me to come along and act as his assistant. The pay for 3 hours work was fantastic for a seventeen-year-old and I jumped at the chance. Unfortunately it only lasted a few months as Luff and I parted company soon after. I had acquired by this time a lovely Lambretta Scooter, paid for mostly out of my "teaching" salary at the college, and one night the fog descended on London in a real "pea-souper", but with the pay so lucrative I was determined to make the journey to Shoreditch. Halfway there, and doing about five miles an hour, I ran into something which turned out to be a road sweeper's cart. This was the first time I was introduced to some very colourful East End language by the road sweeper, not heard again until I joined the Merchant Navy on 3 May 1961.

After some two years, Luff brought a nephew into the business and the writing was on the wall for my departure from Wood Lane. In hindsight I can see that Luff was under pressure to employ a relative, but at the time I was quite upset that I was being ousted to make room for him. This may have been part of an arrangement with another violin repairers, Edward Withers, as I was asked to go and work for them in their Wardour Street workshop the following week.

When Luff died, his whole workshop was moved to a violin dealer in Ealing, I think it was Ealing Strings, and some years ago I visited the showroom and was kindly allowed to have a look at the workshop. Looking at the same bench and tools that I would have used was a unique experience and the memories came flooding back. Although my parting with Luff wasn't on the best of terms, I did have some very good times with him. As I say, I learned a lot from Luff and I am quite proud that some of the violins he produced in the period I was with him have some of my work in their making. I'm not surprised that the instruments now fetch some £10,000 as he made a superb looking and sounding instrument. Luff always involved me in talking to the clients and as a great many of them worked just along Wood Lane at the BBC centre, there was always little insights into what and who was going on in TV. Some of his clients were very accomplished soloists and there were always a few tickets floating about for their recitals, mostly at Wigmore Hall.

Originally named Bechstein Hall, it was built between 1899 and 1901. The renowned British architect Thomas Edward Collcutt was commissioned to design the space. He was also responsible for the Savoy Hotel on The Strand and the Palace Theatre on Cambridge Circus. During the First World War the concert hall was seized, then closed, and in 1916 the hall was sold as alien property at auction for £56,500—a figure considerably short of the £100,000 cost of the building alone. It was then rechristened Wigmore Hall and opened under the new name in 1917.

The recitals by the lesser performers were usually passed to me, so I spent a good many evenings at Wigmore Hall, and I seem to remember telling my date for the evening that the performer was a personal friend of mine, hence the free, very good seats, if we say that it didn't do me any good and leave it at that. So, Luff was a big influence in my formative years and I am very grateful to him for that.

Edward Withers was the founder of the oldest existing violin shop in the UK. The original firm was founded as long ago as 1765, and in 1846, Edward Withers took over the firm, and it continued in the same family for over 120 years until 1969 when the last Edward (they were called "Edward" to perpetuate the name) retired. The shop in Wardour Street had been the home of Withers since 1878 and amongst the great names associated with the shop were the fascinating and brilliant nineteenth century maker John Lott, the French émigré Charles Boullangier, and his namesake Charles Maucotel, to name just a few.

Life in Wardour Street in the Fifties was never dull and I thoroughly enjoyed working there. In fact, I think it played a large part in my education of life. I usually caught the tube to work in the morning and then walked down Lisle Street from the Leicester Square tube. It didn't take me long to realise that all the friendly "good mornings" and offers of "a good time" spoken from doorways as I passed were not what they seemed, but after some time the young and not-so-young ladies of Lisle Street got to know my face (not, I must point out, in a professional way) and the morning greetings became just that. Working in Soho gave me a certain kudos among my old school friends as I was expected to know the places to go and know my way around the more disreputable parts. For the main part, the places to go were the jazz clubs, and we went to them all and saw all the famous traditional jazz musicians of the day, Humphrey Littleton, Chris Barber, Terry Lightfoot, Ken Collier, and the great Acker Bilk, but the one whose club we went to most was Cy Laurie's jazz club. Cy's Club was situated in scruffy Ham Yard, at the junction of Great Windmill and Archer Street; it was entered by going through a set of doors it shared with a strip club and a boxing gym. A dingy staircase descended into a vast basement that was used as a dance rehearsal room during the day. There was little in the way of décor, just hardwood floors and a few dilapidated sofas alongside minimal lighting and a PA system that worked only intermittently. We loved it.

One of the other places we went to was the Friday night dances at the Royal College of Art in Kensington Gore, next to the Albert Hall. I believe that several of the groups who played at these student dances went on to become household names but unfortunately, I can't remember a single one. Remembered with great affection is Eel Pie Island in the River Thames near Twickenham; you had to pay a very small toll to cross the foot bridge, which was privately owned. This was a night out in the country for us, and only after we acquired transport, as it usually meant a very late night and home in the wee small hours, but it was always worth the trip.

People who played at Eel Pie included Cyril Davies, Alexis Korner, Long John Baldry, The Rolling Stones, Rod Stewart, Eric Clapton, John Mayall, Jeff Beck, Jimmy Page, and David Bowie. Eel Pie Island had an even longer pedigree in presenting R&B music. Many major names in British R&B—Cyril Davies's Rhythm & Blues All Stars, Long John Baldry's Hoochie Coochie Men (with Rod Stewart), John Mayall's Bluesbreakers (featuring Eric Clapton), the Tridents (featuring Jeff Beck), and The Who—all performed on the Island between 1962 and 1967.

A place I used go a lot was the Hammersmith Apollo, but in those days, it was called the Hammersmith Odeon and it was mainly used as a cinema. The venue was opened in 1932 and seated nearly 3,500 people. It was designed by Robert Cromie in the Art Deco style. It became a Grade II listed building in 1990. On 28 October 1972, the Giants of Jazz—a supergroup consisting of jazz legends Dizzy Gillespie, Thelonious Monk, drummer Art Blakey, and Sonny Stitt, played the Hammersmith Odeon, and I was lucky enough to be in the audience. In October 1967, an event called Jazz Expo.67 and billed as The Newport Jazz Festival in Britain was held at the Odeon, and the list of jazz stars was legendary. It was staged over eight days and I recall spending quite a large chunk of my wages to go on two of those days. It was a very good investment as on one or other of those days I had the privilege of seeing Miles Davis, Herbie Hancock, Sarah Vaughan, Thelonious Monk, and the great Dave Brubeck.

Soho also gave me a love of various countries' cuisines. Italian was always a favourite but the first taste of Chinese food came one evening when I went out for the night with a school friend, Gerry Tench. In those days, Chinatown wasn't as enormous as it is today, and our restaurant of choice that evening was called The Hong Kong in Shaftsbury Avenue.

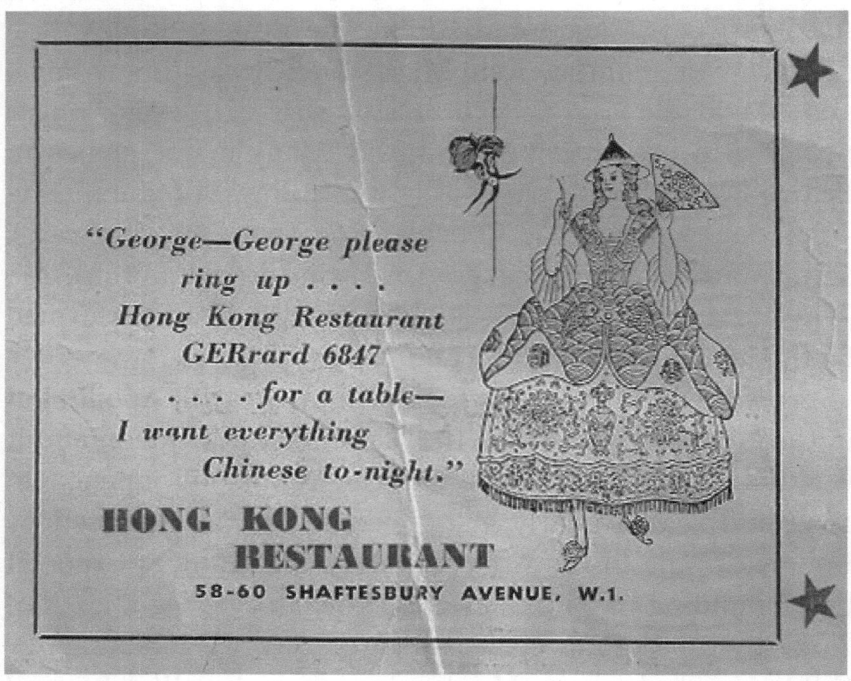

"George—George please
ring up . . . .
Hong Kong Restaurant
GERrard 6847
. . . . . for a table—
I want everything
Chinese to-night."

**HONG KONG RESTAURANT**
58-60 SHAFTESBURY AVENUE, W.1.

I think that first taste of the exotic gave me a love of food that has been with me the rest of my life and is why, for much of my later years, I have been, shall we say, a big lad. Over the years, I think I have tried most types of food and so far, the only things I now refuse are tripe and whelks. One Christmas my parents were out in South Africa visiting my sister which left my brother, wife, Pat, and I to organise and cook Christmas dinner. Pete and I had this great idea to buy a few delicacies from Harrods where at the time I had an account. We brought a few things but couldn't resist getting some crispy grasshoppers and a tin of chocolate covered ants, so I was able to add those delicacies to my list of exotic foods tried, but only the once. Christmas that year wasn't remembered for the food and I was happy to see my mother return shortly after and take control in the kitchen once more.

The first of the school group (Dan, Gerry, Ron, myself, and some friends from other schools) to own a car was Dan Fryer, and as the designated and only driver he took us around town. Strangely, one of the places we frequented was Heathrow, or to be more precise, the bowling hall a short way from the tunnel. Memory does dim with age but I think I'm right in saying that it was probably the first American-style bowling venue in the UK. The Heathrow bit was for a coffee after the bowling and one night there seemed to be hundreds of screaming girls everywhere you looked and we learnt that The Beatles were due to arrive back from their US tour at any moment. None of us (Dan, Gerry, or I) were Beatles fans, so we didn't bother to hang around and left, but as we stopped at the first set of lights past the airport, a big chauffeur-driven car pulled alongside with George Harrison in the back seat. Like the hooligans we were, we followed poor George all the way back to town, waving at him at every stop light until we reached Hyde

Park corner where we once again pulled up level with him. At that point, he wound the window down and said "Come on, lads, I'm really tired. Give us a break." We all leant over out of the window, shook hands, and wished him on his way. I think The Beatles sounded a bit better after that little episode.

***

# Chapter 8

## *My University of Life—on the Ocean Wave*

Working in Soho was great but after a couple of years I started to get a bit restless and my thoughts turned to more exciting places. I had missed out on National Service, being too young at the time before it was abolished, much to my father's dismay, so I thought I would give the RAF the chance to show me the world. I passed a short exam and the interview, but my idea of becoming an Ariel Photographer was dashed at the medical. Because of my short sight, the medics decided that I would need to have the eye examination results reviewed by a specialist. After a week, I was asked to attend the same recruiting office to be told that any flying job was out, but I could be considered as a cook. By that time, I had second thoughts and declined. I consider that this must rank as the shortest time ever to be in the RAF.

The RAF's loss was the Merchant Navy's gain and before long, I had an interview and medical at the Union Castle Shipping Line's offices in the city. On 8 May 1961, accompanied by my father, I got the bus to the Victoria Docks in London's East End to sign on to the MV Warwick Castle. However, the ship was not due to sail for three days, so I had to return home after that first day of "working bye" (getting the ship ready to sail).

The Union Steamship Company was formed at Southampton in 1853, and four years later the line secured a mail contract to South Africa. The well-known "Castle" naming policy was started by a Donald Currie, who initially traded with India in 1862. The merged Union-Castle Mail Steamship Company was registered in 1900.

The Warwick Castle was formerly the Pendennis Castle, which was sold to the Admiralty in 1942 and rebuilt as an aircraft carrier. In 1946, it was re-purchased by Union-Castle and renamed the Warwick Castle. It was scrapped in 1962. The ship's route around Africa was an extensive one and I had the privilege of visiting all these places several times: - Las Palmas - Ascension - St. Helena - Cape Town - Durban – East London – Port Elizabeth – Gibraltar - Genoa - Port Said - Port Suez - Aden - Mombasa - Zanzibar - Dares-Salaam - Beira - Lourenco Marques - Naples – Marseilles.

My first job on board was as an Assistant Steward in the second-class dining saloon. At first, I thought that this would be a piece of cake, but that was before I was told that my day started at six o'clock in the morning and that I had my very own area of floor to clean before helping to bring stores up from the hold to the galley. On that first voyage of two months I went from a rather heavy eleven stone to a skeleton-like nine and a half stone. On my first leave, my mother cried her eyes out when she saw me, but some of her wonderful cooking soon had me back to my fighting weight.

My life has been littered with characters, and the Merchant Navy was no exception as I met, worked, and played with some of the most diverse characters of every nationality imaginable. There was Roger, who was previously a waiter at the Savoy, and Max from Malta who was rumoured to be a very violent criminal wanted back in his own country for unmentionable crimes. I once bought a couple of uniform jackets from Max; he said that there was no hurry to pay, so I didn't, but after a couple of weeks I was advised by another colleague that it was probably wise to pay up sooner than later. The money was in Max's hand that night. My favourite character was a very experienced Italian steward by the name of George who would look at the menu and predict what his passengers would want; he then went to get the meals from the galley which he put in his hot plate. George would then persuade his poor passengers that he had selected the best food on the menu and that the other dishes were not up to standard; furthermore, their wait for other items would be seriously long. I don't know how many people insisted on having something not in the hot plate but George was always away before the others and first in the Crew's mess.

After a very soft working life in Soho, life with Union Castle was a real shock to the system but the camaraderie, the runs ashore, and seeing all these wonderful places more than made up for the long hours and the hard work. I was not a good sailor and never quite got my total sea legs. In fact, returning back to Britain on one voyage through the Bay of Biscay, a force nine gale blow up, galleys were closed, and the passengers were told to remain in their cabins. We lost a lot of crockery and there were a lot of very seasick people on board, including me. I managed to last a day or so but then took to my bunk, not caring if the ship went down or not, until we reached the English Channel. My fellow cabin mates said that they have never quite seen such deep shades of green on someone's face before, but if you have ever been really seasick you will know how I felt. The Warwick Castle was a very small ship by today's standard, being only 17,400 tons against the modern liners of 100,000 tons plus, and she could roll alarmingly in just a heavy swell.

The first country outside the UK I ever saw was Gibraltar and it looked wonderful with the sun shining on the rock and our small tender going off to the port to disembark passengers. Unfortunately, I was on duty during the whole visit and as a consequence never went ashore on that trip, but in the next port of call, Genoa, in Italy, I certainly made up for it. As with all ports around the world, it is the seafarers who know the places to go, the bars to drink in, and where the prettiest girls can be found. Genoa was no exception and I was led by a couple of my more experienced new shipmates to a street near the docks affectionately known to all as "The Dirty Mile". Heading for a bar called The Black Cat and walking along this street packed with bars, I was transported back to Lisle Street, but with far more exotic smells and many more ladies of the night, and what a friendly bunch they were. Suffice to say a good time was had by all.

One of my favourite ports of call was Mombasa in Kenya where a lot of the passengers left the ship, which meant that we got more time off. The day always seemed to follow the same enjoyable pattern. After serving breakfast, a shower and change into a pair of shorts and flip-flops (in those days I seemed to live in white canvas uniform shoes or flip-flops), then a short taxi ride to the Mombasa Seaman's Mission where you could have a few Tuskers beers and a swim in the pool or just relax for a few hours before you hit the town. And hit the town you did; I seem to remember eating a lot of grilled sweetcorn and skewers of unidentifiable meat cooked on an oil drum brazier. All this and much more went on in the front of the Regal Cinema. A good friend, Jag Chadda (much more of him later), was a customs officer around that time, and when the Regal Cinema is mentioned he just rolls his eyes and says, "Not me, Bobby." I recall on one such outing when we were taken to a newly opened nightclub called the Dolphin Club where many G&Ts and much beer was consumed—I actually drank pink gins in those days but can't think why—it seemed to be the sensible thing to do to take off all our clothes and go for a swim in the pool. I don't remember what time I decided to walk back to the ship but I do remember waking up lying in a storm drain at about five o'clock in the morning with several little African kids pointing and laughing their little heads off. It was while the ship was docked in Mombasa that the purser's office organised a fishing competition for the crew. The dock was in deep water so a variety of fish was expected in the catch. However, no one expected what was pulled from the Indian Ocean in the late afternoon: a metre-and-a-half bull shark (*Carcharhinus leucas*). The bull shark is also known as the Zambezi shark and is considered one of the most dangerous sharks in the world since this species has made many attacks on humans. As you would expect, there was quite a bit of commotion going on as the shark was thrashing and snapping about on the deck and no one was prepared to throw it back or kill it. Someone suggested that it would fetch good money in the local market in the morning and that sealed its fate. One of the bosuns brought the discussion to a halt when, with the aid of a large sledge hammer, he despatched the shark. There was a twist to this story: when the two seaman who caught the shark went to collect it from the deck the next morning, it had vanished. Rumours were rife, but the most plausible was that it had been spirited away by some of the locals who had been taken on to paint some of the ship, leaving two very angry members of the crew.

Another favourite port was Cape Town where we were transported to the city centre by rickshaws pulled by members of the Zulu Nation dressed in full tribal regalia. When you reached your destination, the guys would jump very high in the air, tipping the rickshaw backwards. The less informed thought this was all part of the Cape Town experience but our South African shipmates would say that this was to see if any loose change could be forced to roll out of your pocket on to the seat. Those same South African mates first put me onto one of the best, and most potent, drinks I have ever come across, the Brandy Square. This consists of a measure of brandy and one of white port, topped up with ginger ale and served with a big wedge of lemon—wonderful. Beira and Lourenco Marques, in what was then Portuguese East Africa, were great places to spend a couple of hours sitting outside a bar with a few beers. The waiters always served a small plate of nuts, olives, and prawns with each beer, which made the experience even more enjoyable.

One experience I wouldn't have missed for the world was a stop off at St Helena. Part of the British Overseas Territory, St Helena measures about sixteen by eight kilometres. One of the most remote islands in the world, it was for centuries an important stopover for ships sailing to Europe from Asia and South Africa. Napoleon was imprisoned there in exile and died there in 1821. Until very recently, the only way to get to St Helena was by sea, which meant a five-night voyage from Cape Town, and the only ships sailing that route at the time was the Union Castle Line. But in 2017, one of humanity's most isolated out-posts joined the twenty-first century and opened what has been described as "the world's most useless airport". With the opening of the airport and the Napoleon connection to the island, the island's legislative council will be hoping for a steady stream of French tourists wanting to see Longwood house, Napoleon's residence for his last six years. The house is a French estate, bought by Napoleon III for £7,000 in 1858. I was very privileged during my afternoon visit to the island to meet Jonathan, St Helena's oldest resident, who seemed more than happy for me to give him a friendly slap on the back. Jonathan is thought to be 183+ years old and is, of course, a tortoise. It was really strange thinking that I was walking on the same paths that Napoleon had tread. Although an enemy of Britain, it can't be denied that he was one of history's great legends.

My idea before joining the Merchant Navy was to try and see a bit of the world, and so I completed two trips on the Warwick Castle before parting company with Union Castle and signing up with P&O. In those days, different shipping lines had set areas of the world in which they operated with their ships carrying people to a particular destination rather than just cruising. Joining P&O in the Sixties was a big step up as the crew of P&O ships considered themselves to be the guards of the sea. The move gave me a whole new part of the world to explore and on 8 January 1962 I joined the SS Iberia at Tilbury Docks for a four-month voyage to New Zealand. Originally a constituent of the Peninsular and Oriental Steam Navigation Company, P&O is the oldest cruise line in the world, having operated the world's first passenger ships in the early nineteenth century.

On joining the Iberia, I had been promoted to the first-class dining saloon and shared a cabin with only two other people rather than the three on the Warwick Castle. Although I was nineteen years old, this was a different time from today; I was still somewhat naive in the ways of the world. On being shown my cabin, I couldn't help noticing that of the three bunks, two were covered in the normal P&O bedding but one was decked out in a red silk bedspread and matching curtains. When I asked, "Why the difference?" I was told, "Oh, that's Rachael's bunk!"

Such was my naivety at the time, I genuinely thought, "Great, mixed cabins!", but of course they weren't. Rachael turned out to be 6 feet 3 inches, built like a brick outhouse with an awful yellow dye job and the campest manner I had ever at the time seen. Rachael looked after his two much younger cabin mates like a mother hen and was always on hand to offer advice on where to go and which bars to visit, although some of his choices were best avoided! On one occasion, going ashore in Naples, myself and two friends were making our way out of the dock gates when we spotted Rachael coming the other way in some state. He was bleeding from the mouth and his clothes were torn. Very concerned, we rushed up to him and asked what had happened. He said, "I've been attacked, dear."

Three thugs had set about him in one of Naples less salubrious areas but luckily hadn't managed to relieve him of his money or Seaman's book. We helped him back to the ship and made sure he was okay before continuing our night out. One of these friends, a great guy called Theo, was Swiss and as such could speak and read Italian and was in the habit of getting a local newspaper when he could get his hands on one. This was such a day, and he could hardly contain his excitement to tell us of a story that appeared in that mornings edition of *Corriere di Napoli*. It appeared that the police were looking for a large tall blond man who was flamboyantly dressed and had beaten three young Italian men, putting one in hospital. We certainly couldn't think who that man may have been, but speculation came to an end that evening when the ship sailed.

Life on the Iberia was far more civilised than with Union Castle. For one thing, I didn't have to load stores or clean decks and the crew accommodation was much better and although classed as a hanging offence, we usually chose from the first-class passenger menu, ordered one more than was needed for the passengers, and took it to the crew mess to eat. During my time with P&O I experienced some great meals which gave me a lifelong appreciation of fine food. My Swiss friend Theo and I usually worked the same duties and had the same free time so we normally went ashore together. One run ashore that sticks in my mind was Athens where we hired a scooter and toured the sights. The sight of the Parthenon as we rode up towards it was one I shall never forget. It was the first such structure I had ever seen and to my mind is still the most impressive. The Parthenon is a former temple dedicated to the goddess Athena, whom the people of Athens considered their patron. It is the most important surviving building of classical Greece and one of the world's greatest cultural monuments. Unfortunately, on our way back to the ship, the scooter broke down, but with the help of a friendly amateur mechanic we were soon speeding back and arrived in time for the dinner service.

The most charismatic man I had ever met at that time was one Gwyn Harding, a Welshman from Llandudno. A former civil servant with the Ministry of Agriculture, he was the ship's Doctors' Steward and a man full of schemes on how to get rich quick. Another prolific drinker who also liked a wager, and one such wager was that he would drink a full pint of anything put in a pint glass, I would not have believed this had I not seen it with my own eyes. The rules of the bet were that he should down the pint in one go but with no time imposed and not be sick for at least one hour afterwards. I can't tell you the full contents of that pint; suffice it to say there were at least five different spirits and a small amount of Guinness to make him bring the whole lot up. Word had spread around the ship and a lot of cash was being waged; Gwyn took on a large proportion of the bets himself and didn't seem to acknowledge that this could kill him. The corridor outside his cabin was packed with every one thinking they would be a bit richer by that evening. The concoction was mixed, and Gwyn stood up to drink. Very slowly the potent mix disappeared down Gwyn's throat until the glass was empty. Gwyn looked a bit dazed and staggered to the heads, wobbled about a bit in front of one, and raised the hopes of the assembled spectators. But he wasn't sick and after five minutes or so staggered back to his cabin and to the sound of groans from the onlookers, promptly passed out on his bunk. Gwyn was missing from his duties the next day but won over £100 that afternoon and I'm sure did unimaginable damage to his health. One of Gwyn's get-rich-quick schemes was to try and bring ashore in the UK a large quantity of cigarettes to resell at a profit. Given that cigarettes at crew prices in the Sixties were very low, the scheme was feasible but of course highly illegal. Gwyn's idea was to pack a large suitcase with cigarettes and include it in the ship doctor's baggage, and as it was he who carried the bags ashore, he felt that no customs officer would search a doctor's case. How wrong he was, as the doc was stopped but of course denied the that suitcase was his. Gwyn stated that it was outside the doctor's cabin so he naturally thought it was to be taken landside. The cigarettes were confiscated but no one was fined. I remained friends with Gwyn after we both left the Navy. The crew price of cigarettes at the time was nine old shillings for two hundred but the duty was raised and they went up to eleven shillings. I said that I'm not paying that price and promptly gave up this unhealthy habit for the rest of my life.

After each voyage, three of us, Gwyn Harding, Rodger from the Savoy, and myself, always arranged to meet up on the first night of our leave, and the venue was always the same, dog racing at the White City Stadium and off to the Aberdeen Steakhouse in Leicester Square for a good late supper. I was never a great gambler and never lost much money, however I must have inherited a love of racing from my dear old dad because I did like a night out at the dogs. Gwyn and I enjoyed the buzz of the White City and the odd small flutter but Rodger was a serious punter. On one night, we had to pay for his meal because he had a run of bad luck and gambled away the whole of his pay from a two-month voyage. We never saw Rodger again after that night. I presume he went back to sea earlier than he needed to earn more betting money. The White City Stadium was built in the White City area of London for the 1908 Summer Olympics. It hosted swimming, speedway, and a match in the 1966 World Cup. From 1927 until 1984 it was the premier venue for greyhound racing, hosting the English Greyhound Derby. The stadium was demolished in 1985.

In those far distant days I was quite a snappy dresser with both handmade shirts as well as suits. All this was possible due to the ship calling at Hong Kong. The port before reaching Honk Kong was Singapore, where a Hong Kong tailor, who we called Mr Nathan because his shop was in Nathan Road, and an assistant came aboard to take orders. It was obviously worth his while to pay for his passage back to Hong Kong and measure up anyone wanting a suit or shirt. He would radio the orders and measurements back to his shop and a few days later when you docked in Hong Kong, Mr Nathan would be waiting for your first fitting and the next day your beautifully fitted suit would be delivered to the ship. I think I had two suits and a blazer made, the suits in a silk mohair in Mod style and the shirts with cutaway collars and monogrammed on the front. I must have thought I looked a million dollars as all my old school friends were still wearing Burton suits that looked like they were made for other people—unkind but true. I have since had shirts made while on holiday in Bangkok but they never came up to the quality and style of Mr Nathan.

One port I will always remember was San Francisco, mainly for three reasons. One, I bought my first real pair of jeans direct from the Levi shop where they were made (Levi Strauss was founded in San Francisco in 1853). In keeping with the trendy practice of the day, I got a pair one size too big. Now, at home you got into your jeans, filled up the bath, sat in it, and hoped they moulded to your shape, but in the crew quarters this wasn't an option and so one tied them to a length of strong rope and dangled them out of the porthole into the sea overnight. This not only shrunk them but gave a nice faded look. It's not known how many pairs of jeans were lost at sea but they certainly looked the business on runs ashore. The second reason I remember the port was that I was thrown off a San Francisco tram; well, asked to get off, and all because I was eating a hot dog while travelling. And the third memorable event occurred when a group of us went out one night to a bar/nightclub. As I was the only one in the party under twenty-one, I was not allowed in the main bar and had to spend the night in a side room on my own without a clear view of the stage and drinking Coke all night. Believe I missed Ella Fitzgerald, and I have hated Coke ever since.

Another P&O ship I briefly served on was The Orcades, a small passenger liner that had just started to cruise rather than transport people. I signed off that ship in August 1962 and started to plan a voyage with my best schoolmate, Ron Parissien, but not everything in life turns out as you plan. Ron had just left the Royal Navy due to him losing his trigger finger and, being a gunner, he was able to leave before his service ended. The plan was for both of us to join the same ship and sail to more exotic places together. In the time I had been in the MN I had sailed many more sea miles than Ron and he wanted to experience real world travel. The first problem was that Ron could only get a job as deck crew on Shell tankers, so I duly applied to Shell and was taken on as a crew mess man on the M.S. Amastra. I joined the ship on 29 August 1962 at Immingham and immediately realised that I had made an almighty mistake and the worst part was that Ron had been assigned a different ship and was on his way to the Persian Gulf. When you signed ships articles in those days you could only sign off the vessel when it returned to British waters. Poor Ron spent the next eight months in the heat of the Gulf with only a Coke machine supplying something to drink. I on the other hand was very lucky in that the Amastra called in at Glasgow before docking in Liverpool to discharge oil, and one week after I had sailed from Immingham I signed off and took the Mersey ferry across to Liverpool for the first train back to my beloved London. Five years after I left the Amastra it was bombed in Vietnam, and I can just see my old cabin from the photos of the half-sunk ship.

Leaving Shell was the end of my Merchant Navy career and I couldn't think of what would come next. Unfortunately, I still didn't know what I wanted to do after I left school.

In recent years I have been on a number of cruises, thankfully as a passenger, sailing with Holland America, Norwegian Line, Princess, Celebrity, Royal Caribbean, Cunard, and P&O. On one of the trips with P&O, I approached the Purser's Office (now sadly called the Customer Service desk) to ask, as a former employee of the line, if I could see the crew's quarters. A day later I received a phone call to say I had been assigned an assistant customer service officer to show me around below decks. To say that I was surprised during the inspection was the understatement of the year. I was totally unprepared for the facilities and conditions I was shown. Several crew bars, lounge areas with a large LED TV screen, single and double cabins, a swimming pool, and, to top it all, a jacuzzi. It was light years away from my four-in-a-cabin and very small crew mess. Life on the ocean wave has certainly changed a bit! One thing that is hard to get one's head around is the statistics of a present-day cruise in terms of numbers. A ship of some 90,000 tons uses on average 15,225 pool towels on a seven-day cruise, sheets required on the same sailing: 11,600, bars of soap used in a year: 5,000,000, and the number of chocolates placed on pillows in a year: 15,000,000. Useless stats, I know, but no less impressive.

*Warwick Castle*

*M.S. Amastra*

*I remember that I had to hold onto the chair,*
*and it wasn't because of the ship's motion.*

***

# Chapter 9

## *Two Years in Hospital—but They Paid Me*

After leaving the Merchant Navy, I got a job in the catering department of St George's Hospital, Hyde Park Corner, as an assistant to the butcher, Steve, who turned out to be the most miserable person I had ever met.

However, after working together for a few weeks we got along famously and he taught me the skills of his ancient trade. Steve was an officer's batman during World War II and accompanied the officer to Belsen, the Nazi concentration camp. When it was liberated on 15 April 1945, by the British 11th Armoured Division, Steve was tasked in taking photographs of the appalling sights they found, and still had some of the original pictures which he showed me, and I have never forgotten those dreadful scenes.

The butcher's department at the hospital was set in the large storeroom run by two of the funniest men one could wish to meet, Bill and George. This comic pair was notorious in the hospital for their practical jokes and their singing using their own lyrics, "Delia, oh, Delia, I'll feel you tonight."

These, of course, were not the original lyrics from *The Merry Widow*. Nurses who came down to the stores to collect items for the wards lived in fear of embarrassment but there was never any harm meant, and all seemed to take it well. George had just bought himself a car, despite only recently learning to drive; he had elected my help to sit in the seat as the qualified driver. I was also allowed to use the car after dropping him off after work. This was great for me as I got to use the car most days, a big old Ford. Working at St George's situated at Hyde Park Corner held no fear for me driving this big old car to the hospital as a few months prior to passing my test, I was taught to drive by an instructor who always seemed to arrange to pick me up for the lesson at my place of work, and I had to drive around Hyde Park Corner and back to Notting Hill. In hindsight, it was the best grounding I could have wished for. St George's Hospital was established in 1733 in a country home built in 1719 by James Lane, 2nd Viscount Lanesborough. In 1826, the trustees of St George's commissioned William Wilkins to design a new hospital. Wilkins was also the architect for the National Gallery in Trafalgar Square and University College. This building was completed in the early 1830s. This historic building has now been carefully restored during an extensive four-year project (1988–1991) and transformed into a magnificent hotel which takes the name of the former Lanesborough House on this site.

Working in the basement store room where the butcher's shop and the cold room were located, and on occasions the kitchens on the top floor, I saw quite a lot of the medical staff. One that springs to mind was a very tall and slim gentleman (think Christopher Lee in his famous role, but without the fangs) who was in charge of the hospital mortuary. The happiest man you could wish to meet, always humming a tune and with a smile for everyone. One morning, Bill the storeman said that he had forgotten to include a jar of coffee in the mortuary supplies order, and as I was just about to go to the kitchens, would I be so kind as to drop the jar off on my way? I think I went through the whole range of emotions. I was curious to see the mortuary but would rather give the sight of what I may find on the slabs a miss. With great trepidation, I knocked on the mortuary door and was told to enter only to find "Mr Lee" sitting by one of the examination tables reading a book and eating his sandwiches. There was no one occupying the other tables but my courage failed me and I declined the offer of a coffee and fled.

Situated next to the storeroom was the vegetable preparation room, where Jack was in charge over three other men. Friendly enough, he was something of a man of mystery: jet black (dyed) hair and the thinnest pencil moustache you ever saw to match. Every night, when the other staff had left, Jack would fill one of the large preparation sinks, strip to the waist, and wash. Half an hour later, Jack would leave the hospital dressed to kill. No one knew anything about his home life or where he disappeared to at night, but bright and early the next morning, Jack would be dressed in his work clothes ready to start another day. One of Jack's staff was also a bit strange. I will call him Lennie (think of the character in John Steinbeck's *Of Mice and Men*). One Christmas, someone in the veg prep department acquired a large quantity of medical alcohol and thought it a good idea to hold a small party. Mixed with a great many bottles of Coca-Cola it was still lethal but the men from the veg prep were hardened drinkers and none more so than Lennie. The brew was far too powerful for me and I declined their kind offer to partake, but I was told the next day that the party went on until the small hours and Lennie saw off more than his fair share of the cocktail. Jack arrived a little late the next morning only to find that he only had one other to help him prepare the veg for the next twenty-four hours. I don't think that many patients got their five-a-day that day. However, we were all worried about Lennie as he hadn't turned up for work for three days after the party. Just on the point where we were about to call the police, he appeared and all he said was "Great party."

Life on the ocean wave was far better paid than life in the NHS, so when the offer from the bread/cake delivery man (George) came, to help him with his busy Saturday deliveries, I jumped at the chance. The company of course was Lyons and for the next few months I met up with George at their distribution centre near the Olympia, Kensington. George was a lovely man; we got along famously and I enjoyed the job, to say nothing of the "leftover" cakes I took home. One delivery I really looked forward to was at South Ruislip USAF Base. I couldn't believe the facilities they had: a three-lane bowling alley, a hotdog and burger café, and enough food to feed half of London, but the best thing was their coffee, and I drank gallons.

The hospital had one great thing going for it, The Grenadier, a pub that was only a few hundred yards out of the back door. Originally built in 1720 as the officers' mess for a regiment of foot guards, The Grenadier became a licensed premise in 1818 to serve as The Guardsman Public House; it was later renamed The Grenadier. It was famously known as the Duke of Wellington's officers' mess and was frequented by King George IV. The pub is said to be haunted by a young guardsman, nicknamed Cedric, who was murdered there, but the only spirits I ever saw were the ones in the optics. It was said that there was a telephone extension from the hospital to the pub to recall any doctor who was enjoying a liquid lunch. I had many a happy hour in The Grenadier but the last time I visited, it appeared that the entrance in the mews at the back of the old St Georges was impassable and I had to walk a long way around to reach it.

It was at St George's that I met Herbert, a chef who was German and very camp. Possibly because I had been in the Merchant Navy, or just that I was new to the hospital, we became friends and he soon met Pat, my wife, and I met his partner, Richard. I didn't think that this pair were the stereotypical gay couple; as I said, Herbert was very flamboyant and camp and Richard was quite straight, having served in the Gibraltarian Army. His father was Gibraltarian, his mother was French, and Richard spoke both Spanish and French as well as English. He was a very cool guy; smoked Gauloises, read *Le Monde*, and had his hair cut at the Green Park Hotel, where he worked. The couple had been together for some years and had worked together as chef and steward on a private yacht in the south of France. Richard was always shouting at Herbert to "get some of that make-up off" and "if I wanted a woman, I would go out and get one". We loved their company and spent many a happy hour getting drunk in one or other of their dubious clubs in Soho. One of the best times I ever spent in Paris was when we went with them to visit Richard's mother who showed us the real French capital.

I thoroughly enjoyed my time at St George's but after some eighteen months the urge for change reared up again and I applied for a job in the catering department of The London Hospital, Whitechapel.

The Royal London Hospital was founded in September 1740 and was originally named The London Infirmary. The name changed to The London Hospital in 1748 and then to The Royal London Hospital in 1980 when the Queen came to visit and gave it the added "Royal". The hospital is the base for London's Air Ambulance, operating out of a rooftop helipad. Joseph Merrick, known as the "Elephant Man", spent the last few years of his life at The Royal London Hospital, and his mounted skeleton is currently housed at the Medical School but is not on public display.

This was a big opportunity for me as the job was for a catering assistant in the office. The London Hospital at the time bought all its requirements directly, from cornflakes to theatre equipment, and this was all ordered by the catering department. It came as a bit of a shock when I was called for an interview, which went quite well, and an even bigger shock when I was offered the position. By the time I got the notification of the job offer, I had begun to have second thoughts. The journey to Whitechapel, for one; the pay was slightly less than I was earning at St George's but to be perfectly honest I had my doubts that I was up to the work and eventually turned it down, an action I often think was one of the bigger mistakes in my life. I was still looking for a career change when a short time after I spotted a notice at the hospital asking for student operating theatre technicians to train at St Thomas' Hospital in Lambeth.

St Thomas' Hospital is a large NHS teaching hospital in Central London. Administratively part of Guy's Hospital and King's College Hospital and originally located in Southwark but based in Lambeth since 1871, the hospital has provided healthcare freely or under charitable auspices since the twelfth century. It is one of London's most famous hospitals, associated with names such as Florence Nightingale and Sir Harold Ridley. It is a prominent London landmark, largely due to its location on the opposite bank of the River Thames to the Houses of Parliament.

Amazingly, they didn't ask for any qualifications or medical experience. Now this was more like it, swaggering around in scrubs impressing young nurses and helping to mend the sick. Once again, how wrong I was. Again, I applied, and I think that because I was already working in the NHS, I was taken on for a twelve-month trial. In today's world where many nurses have a degree, this is unbelievable, but there I was on my first day getting a welcome talk by one of the theatre sisters who outlined what my next few weeks would be like. The first week was a series of talks and lectures, most of which went right over my head, but it gave me the opportunity to talk with my fellow students, all young female trainee nurses. The first big shock came when I had to watch an operation. I had been warned that my first sight of blood may upset me and I could faint, but I was not expecting the first op to be on a very young baby. I didn't faint but as the surgeon made his first cut I felt decidedly queasy. Then came the day when I had to actually do something and I was shown how the autoclave worked and spent the day putting trays of bloody clamps, forceps, and assorted surgical equipment in and out of a very hot machine. An autoclave is a pressure chamber used to sterilize equipment and supplies by subjecting them to high pressure saturated steam at 121°C (249°F) for around 15–20 minutes depending on the size of the load and the contents.

On other days, I worked in the operating theatre, mostly weighing the used swabs to let the surgeon know how much blood the patient had lost, but by the end of four months I was told to scrub up to help the anaesthetist on the Boyle's machine.

The original concept of Boyle's machine was invented by the British anaesthetist Henry Boyle (1875–1941) in 1917. Prior to this time, anaesthetists often carried all their equipment with them, but the development of heavy, bulky cylinder storage and increasingly elaborate airway equipment meant that this was no longer practical for most circumstances. The anaesthetic machine is usually mounted on anti-static wheels for convenient transportation. I even got to assist in a simple tonsillectomy where I handed the surgeon the instruments. All went well until he asked me to cut the end of the suture tying the poor patient's tonsils, and in my green and nervous state I of course cut the wrong one. I was beginning to enjoy the work and the atmosphere in the theatre, but found it hard to comply with the working hours. Surgeons are dedicated men and woman who thought nothing of fitting another case in at the end of their list, and of course when things don't go to plan in an operating theatre everyone stays to the end. I lost count of the number of girlfriends who packed me in after I failed to show for a date. After some six months, I decided that I wasn't as dedicated to the medical profession as I thought I was, and I handed in my notice and subsequently exited from the NHS. However, my time in both parts of the NHS left me with a huge respect and admiration for the service and all the dedicated people who work in it.

My own stays in various hospitals have increased in later life and to date I have racked up: one gall bladder removal (laparoscopic), two glaucoma and two cataract ops, two total knee replacements, and one skin graph. My laparoscopic procedure was carried out by a wonderful old surgeon who was very well-known in Cheshire, John Clegg. Mr Clegg was of the old school of surgeons who didn't go in for keyhole surgery, resulting in a five-inch scar on my stomach. When I retired in 2002, I enrolled on a year's computer course, ECDL, at the local college, and lo and behold John Clegg was a fellow student. John was writing a book and needed the computer skills to do this, but by this time he wasn't the steady-handed user of a scalpel he once was. The rest of the class was mightily reassured to learn that he too was retired. It was time to put my medical career to one side and find another path in life. When I told my parents that I was joining the Civil Service they were as pleased as punch that I was at last getting, as my dad said, a "proper job".

\*\*\*

# Chapter 10

## *Marriage—Well, We All Make Mistakes*

My first real girlfriend was a lovely, kind, and good-natured young lady called Vickie, who I treated rather badly. We met when both our mothers and their children were on holiday at a holiday camp in Leysdown on the Isle of Sheppey. Being both the same age and probably the only teenagers in the camp, we got on very well. Like most young people of that age we were into pop music. Cliff Richards had a hit that summer with Living Doll. We entered and won a jive contest and become good friends. Vickie lived near Kentish Town so we only saw each other about once a week, meeting up near Oxford Street and generally going to the pictures or for a coffee. As the relationship grew, Vickie became pregnant, and on 9 February 1964, my beautiful little daughter Jacqueline Andrea was born. A horrible time for both of us, as a single mother was not acceptable in the early Sixties and I knew in my heart of hearts that we couldn't make a go of it. Any thoughts of a possible marriage were blown apart when I learnt, I seem to remember from her mother, that while I had been at sea, Vickie had been seeing an old school friend of mine, but by this time and without my blessing, the baby had been adopted. I am still deeply sad and ashamed of that episode in my life and how badly I treated Vickie. I think about Jacqueline quite often and hope and pray that she has had a good life and is well and happy. I would love to know how her life has been, but we pay for our actions and I guess I never will. Who knows, I may have famous grandchildren.

One Saturday evening, Dan, Gerry, and I ended up in South Kensington at a café called The Hayloft. The night proved to be a momentous one as both Dan and I met our first wives there, both ironically called Patricia. Pat and I lived together for a while in the basement flat of a friend of hers, Jessica, in a really upmarket Knightsbridge location, Ennismore Gardens. Entry to the flat was via the very impressive front door and down one floor to the basement in the even more impressive house lift. I loved to see our friends' faces as they visited us for the first time. Unfortunately, the apartment, being a one room with kitchen and bathroom, didn't quite live up to the stately entrance. However, we did have neighbours who were impressive: Charles Gray, the actor (his work included the *James Bond* movies) lived across the road, and the legendary Dusty Springfield lived next door. I once pushed an invitation through her letterbox to a party we were giving but alas, she must have been busy on that night. Ava Gardner lived and died at number 34 and the actor Jack Hawkins also lived there. There have been many other notable characters listed as living in the Gardens but I'm afraid that I am not amongst them.

Pat was a fully trained nursery nurse (another rather spooky similarity with Alan Johnson, as his first wife was also a nursery nurse) and as such was much in demand. In our time living in London she worked for some pretty powerful families and coincidently did some babysitting for the Marquis of Queensberry, who was Professor of Ceramics at the Royal College of Art at the time. When we decided to get married, to secure the Knightsbridge apartment after Jessica moved out, it was because of the address that the Registry Office we were obliged to use was the famous

Caxton Hall. The list of people who tied the knot here is legendary: Diana Dors, Elizabeth Taylor, Peter Sellers, Roger Moore, Joan Collins, George Harrison, and Ringo Starr, among others. We spent our honeymoon in Paris, which wasn't the great romantic time we had envisaged. At the stroke of midnight, my new wife was snoring her head off and I was out on the Champs-Élysées looking for somewhere to get a bite to eat.

Years later, I met and fell head over heels for Linda, my lovely wife. My first marriage break-up was entirely my fault, a fact that I'm not proud of, but I do know that within a very short time Pat had met someone new; I only hope that she found some of the happiness that I have.

When I first started to go out with Linda, her best friend, Val, told me that a few years before she joined the Civil Service she had been a model for Marks & Spencer. She certainly had the looks, but surely all models are six foot tall, were they not? Linda herself was rather reluctant to talk about this past part of her life but later told me that at seventeen she had been thrilled to be asked to model for M&S but, being very petite, she was horrified to learn that they wanted her to model clothes for ages twelve to fifteen years, and petrified that her friends would find out that she was back in gymslips again.

The day I got the better of James Bond—it came when Linda and I were first seeing each other. We used to meet up for lunch from time to time at a lovely old pub in Frodsham called The Ring O' Bells, and on one such occasion we were constantly been interrupted and disturbed by James Bond making a nuisance of himself. After a while I had had enough of this behaviour and told him in no uncertain terms to bog off. He left without a word. The James Bond I speak of was Daniel Craig, and at the time he was about five years old. The landlord of the pub was his father.

It was at Runcorn in the Department of Employment that I met my wife Linda and where my first marriage began to break up. Linda and I met playing badminton in the local Runcorn Scout/Army Cadet hall. She always wore the shortest of shorts with an embroidered butterfly on the rear and she looked stunning, but come to that, she still does. Soon after my first marriage broke up, Linda and I moved in together to a small flat near the Runcorn Shopping City, which wasn't the nicest of areas, and we soon moved to a lovely housing association property, Powell's Orchard, just near the River Dee in Chester. We loved that place and one of the great joys in those days was to walk by the river into Chester on Saturday to have lunch at The Grosvenor Hotel, which in those far off days was a huge buffet. Chester and The Grosvenor Hotel are still two of my favourite places in the world and there are not many weeks go by when we don't visit both, although nowadays it's just for coffee.

While living in Chester, my transfer to the Immigration Service came through and the commute to Manchester Airport became a pain, and so the hunt for somewhere nearer to buy was on. The Civil Service rules on giving help to move on transferring to another location, called a Public Expenses Transfer, are, or were at the time, that you had to live forty miles or more away from your new work place. Powell's Orchard to Manchester Airport is approximately 47 miles, so I was lucky enough to get a government loan and moving expenses to enable us to move twelve miles inside the forty-mile limit to our first real house on Delamere Park. We fell for a lovely new two-bedroom townhouse on the estate and approached the selling agent, a fearsome lady called Mrs Johnson (more on Mrs J in chapter 19)

Linda started to climb the promotion ladder and while working for the Learning and Skills Council she was asked to go to Portugal to help various industries with their development and training. She was partnered on this mission by a friend and work colleague, Brian Wilks. While they were in a town called Amarante, I arranged with Brian's wife, Sandra, to join them for a long weekend. We all had some lovely meals together and accompanied them on some of their visits to vineyards and Port wine-making farms. It was at one such farm that we saw huge stainless-steel vats and new modern equipment which was acquired with EU money, but in one corner we spotted a very old grape press and vat. When I asked the owner what this old equipment was for he replied, "That's where we make our own Port."

To back his claim that they produced the best white Port in Portugal, he gave us a couple of bottles to try. He was right; it was nectar, and I only wish that it was on sale in this country.

When I returned with Sandra and passed through passport control it caused quite a stir, and the rumour mongers were in full cry. "Did you see that Rob Howe? He's been away with another woman," etc. Linda continued her rise in the promotion stakes and later became the Chief Executive at Macclesfield Business Link, formally Macclesfield Chamber of Commerce.

One of the small perks for me to come out of Linda's job was the dinners and functions she was invited to and to which I tagged along. ICI always held their Christmas dinners at Astra Zeneca headquarters in Cheshire. A black-tie affair with lots of local dignitaries attending and splendid after-dinner speakers. Two regulars on those evenings were the husband and wife MPs, the Hamiltons. I could say a lot more, but noting their success in court proceedings, I will hold my tongue. A function we went to in Liverpool, an Investors in People event, was hosted and compared by Gyles Brandreth. An MP at the time, he was incredible, and he held the difficult audience in the palm of his hand, even putting down some rather inebriated businessmen in witty but sarcastic one-liners. He is not the clown he sometimes comes across. Those evenings sometimes included a night's stay in the hotel where the function was being held and on some of those occasions, usually award ceremonies, I tended to elect to stay in the room and enjoy the hotel's room service and movie channels. I rather miss that side of her work; I was able to brush up on my small talk, and I must confess that after liberal amounts of champagne, I got rather good at chatting up the "other halves".

When Linda and I had been together for some ten years and we had agreed that the sound of tiny feet was not going to be an option, I thought that I would do the decent thing and have "the snip". I arranged to have the procedure done privately and made an appointment with the clinic in St John's Street, Manchester. The doctor carrying out the procedure was an Indian gentleman and judging by his accent was not British-born. Now I am perfectly okay with this, however I had, at the time, just refused an Indian family who didn't qualify for entry and was very much aware that this gentleman was Indian and, more to the point, had my future in his hands, so when he asked me what I did for a living I very nervously said, "Oh, something boring in the Civil Service," but my mind was screaming "I'm not in the Immigration Service, honest."

The moment passed and after a short while I was able to do a John Wayne walk back to the car.

After twenty-eight years together, Linda and I decided we should get married. I'd love to say that the decision was born out of romance, but it was for a far more important reason—to stop the Treasury getting its hands on one of our pensions in the event of one of us passing away. Although the reasons were a bit practical, the date and venue for our nuptials were very romantic. We arranged to get married the day before the millennium on the Isle of Skye. The actual wedding ceremony was rather strange as the registry office is a room in the registrar's house in Portree. The registrar's husband and daughter acted as witnesses and they tried to make the ceremony special, but to enter the room to the sound of Elvis singing "Love Me Tender" is not really something we would have chosen, however any disappointment we may have had over the setting was cancelled out by the wonderful view from the picture window.

Where and who do you stay with on one's honeymoon on the Isle of Skye, as well as cerebrating the millennium? Only one option, really: with Lord and Lady Macdonald at Kinloch Lodge. The food has to be very good and that's no problem as Claire Macdonald is a renowned cook and author of over twelve bestselling cookbooks. It certainly did not disappoint; the food was incredible, and the Macdonalds wonderful hosts. Godfrey James Macdonald of Macdonald, eighth Lord Macdonald, is the high chief of Clan Donald. Godfrey, as we were encouraged to call him, organised walks around the lodge, and on New Year's Eve they held a traditional ceilidh dance with a caller for the Scottish dancing. The whole of the Macdonald family was there to bring in the new century, and the fireworks over the sea loch at midnight was something we will never forget.

We hadn't told any of our family in Aberdeen of the wedding, and after our stay at Kinloch Lodge, we drove across to my in-laws who live in Banchory. On hearing that we had just got married, my lovely mother-in-law, Iris, said "Linda, you're not pregnant, are you?"

Not impossible, but at fifty-two, highly improbable. We took the whole family out for a celebratory meal and a few days later returned to Cheshire with our pensions now safely secured from the Treasury's clutches.

Linda coming from Aberdeen means we visit Scotland several times a year, to family and for city breaks in Edinburgh, etc. The very first time I went to Aberdeen was to celebrate the New Year (Hogmanay), and I'm afraid I rather disgraced myself. In England, we tend to celebrate in the run up to midnight, but the tradition in Scotland is to celebrate the New Year after the bells at midnight. So that first time I met Linda's family I had been drinking from the early evening, and by midnight I was slumped on a chair fast asleep, missing the party. I think the family thought, *what on earth has Linda dragged up here? He's such a lightweight.* I have to say that I think I have "scotched" that opinion over the past few years.

In the early Nineties, Gleneagles, the very famous hotel, used to have a great reduction in their prices just after the New Year and we were able to go and stay for a few nights. During that time, I was still riding on a regular basis and Gleneagles had the Mark Phillips Riding School. I couldn't resist booking a hack, and of course Linda had to come as well, so early one morning we turned up at the stables to be given a short test to see that we could in fact get on a horse facing the right way. There were about twelve of us with varying degrees of riding skill and the horses seemed quite controlled, gently circling the ménage. However, the instructor had failed to tell us that due to the bad weather, the horses had not been outside for almost two weeks. When the doors opened to the Scottish countryside, the horses took off en masse like the Charge of the Light

Brigade. There were riders falling off, some disappearing in the distance, and others holding on for grim death with the poor instructor shouting to "turn your horse—turn your horse". Linda and I were very lucky to have two of the more docile creatures, and after fifty yards or so managed to turn our mounts back to the ménage to finish the session on the lanes around the hotel.

One of my first holidays with Linda could have quite easily been my last. An open-topped sports car (MG Midget) travelling the backroads of France, stopping and pitching our tent in beautiful surroundings, what could possibly go wrong? We got as far as Lyon when my six-month-old Midget broke down on the motorway. Luckily, a very surly and officious policeman stopped to shout at us in very rapid French which we interpreted as "Get that piece of British rubbish off the hard shoulder." However, he did phone his mate, the garage owner, to inform him that there were two British tourists on the hard shoulder who needed to spend a lot of francs to repair their piece of trash called an MG. One and a half hours later, Pierre turned up with his clapped-out old tow truck, and it was then that I learned a gesture that is truly universal. The repair man (I have yet to see a woman do this) while looking at the job in hand, shakes his head and at the same time utters a tutting sound. At that point, you just know that it's time to think of who would consider giving you a second mortgage. Two nights staying in the Hotel de Commerce did nothing to cement our relationship, but we did have some nice meals and as the car was under warranty, MG paid all the parts which had to be shipped from England. As we finally left the garage, Pierre was beside himself with joy to have helped relieve two Brits of some of their lovely pounds, and I began to think that he was in fact a long-lost brother.

The rest of journey to the south went quite smoothly, but for some worrying moments when we began to realise that French campers tend to fill campsites in August, and also it gets rather warm. We happily made it to our reserved site near St Tropez and prepared to enjoy the holiday. I can't remember which came first, the flood or the sunburn, but both were memorable. One night when it had been raining for most of the day, we were woken to the sound of two men trying to dig their way into our tent; very scary until we were told that they were digging trenches around our tent to prevent it from being washed away as the storm was getting wilder. We had pitched our tent on the bottom of a slight hill which didn't help. I think it was two days later that the south of France lived up to its reputation and gave us temperatures in the high thirties. Linda, being from Scotland, had some issues with the tanning process. Completely forgetting that she had to go from blue to white before turning brown, she got very red and had to wear a long cover-up for the next few days. Of course, it wasn't all doom and gloom. We had some great days and one of the most memorable meals I have ever had. We were in St Raphael and just managed to stumble on a much sought-after parking place near the station, where we spotted a very local looking restaurant. Not very original, but it may have been called "The Station Restaurant". The menu looked good, so we went in to be met by a fierce-looking lady with bright orange hair who promptly ordered us to sit in the middle of the restaurant. She then proceeded to remove the menus on the table and, in a torrent of French and arm waving, disappeared into the kitchen. We hadn't ordered a thing, but a nice bottle of white wine was placed on our table followed by a wonderful platter of fruits de mer. Mrs Orange Hair, who was obviously the patron, seemed to be running the restaurant with a rod of iron and telling the other diners what to eat. The fish dish that followed was out of this world, and the cheese, followed by a great crème caramel, was outstanding. I can remember that l'addition was very reasonable and Mrs O.H. saw us off the premises as old friends. The end of the holiday was marked by us having our first major, almost fighting and storming off, row. The problem was trying to find our way around Rouen. We were parked on the side of the road and just as I was about to place my hands around the neck of the "navigator", a car pulled up behind us and a French angel got out and asked if we needed any help. She told us to follow her through the city and she would wave when we were on the right road to Calais. What a wonderful lady; if it hadn't been for her, I may well have spent the next twenty-five years near to where it all started for me—The Scrubs. We have never been camping since and are never likely to in the future, preferring nowadays to sleep at somewhere you can drink the water and they have valet parking.

*Linda as she was when I first met her.*

***

# Chapter 11

## *The Not-So Civil Service*

After some weeks of waiting, my application to join the Civil Service was successful and I was taken on at the Board of Trade in Victoria Street, London, as a photo printer grade two. The work was so soul-destroyingly boring it was a wonder I stuck it, but I am so glad I did. The majority of the work of a grade two photo printer was to collate reports and documents and to make photocopies. To relieve some of that boredom, I started spending my lunch hours at a pub just down Victoria Street in Strutton Ground called The Grafton. This hostelry was the place where Spike Milligan, Peter Sellers, Harry Secombe, and Michael Bentine first started writing *The Goon Show*. The man who lit the blue touch paper for the show was Jimmy Grafton, publican, scriptwriter, and Secombe's manager. He installed a small stage upstairs in the pub, edited the material, and finally nagged a nervous BBC into signing up the gang.

It seemed to go unnoticed that I returned to work half cut and it certainly made the afternoons pass quickly. We were, on occasions, tasked with putting together very large reports, many running to forty or fifty pages. This had to be done by hand with the pages laid out on a very big table and us collating the report by going around the table picking up each page and stapling it at the end. To make this stimulating work slightly less mind-blowing, we conceived a game of timing the rounds with a free tea and sausage roll going to the winner. I can't recall ever winning a round but remember the sausage rolls from a tea trolley that went around the offices as the best ever. My colleagues in the reproduction department of the Board of Trade, once I got to know them, were a great bunch, mainly from the East End of London. I seem to have been lucky in my working life to have worked with so many characters, and this bunch had them in spades. There was Ernie; he lived, worked, and no doubt slept as a cowboy. Ernie dressed as a cowboy and was constantly being told that he wasn't to come to work in string ties with a cow horn waggle, but on his days off he wore the whole outfit. He was part of a like-minded group who rented a field with a hut which they used for re-enactments of Western battles and gun fights. At one point, the group raised enough money to buy an old horse, but unfortunately no one had any knowledge of looking after horses—"They live on grass, don't they?". Sadly, during the first winter, the poor animal passed away due to the lack of nutrients in the grass. I may have mocked Ernie a bit but his band of cowboys did a lot for charity and raised a lot of money with their Western shows for several good causes. There was little Mike, whose father had been a fair ground fighter, Harry and his brother Eric who had both served in the Army, and Philip, who was a composer of classical music. Harry once told me of his experiences during the Suez crisis in 1956 when, as a young conscript, he was part of the invading British forces taking the Suez Canal. On the landing craft, Harry said the NCOs were saying things like "We may not all come back from this," and "Good luck, men. We will see to the injured after the battle," etc. So, when the front of the landing craft came down, naturally enough, Harry was close to soiling his combats, but what greeted them wasn't bloodthirsty Egyptians but locals offering to sell them postcards of a dubious nature. Eric had been a physical trainer in the Army and was very fit. On one occasion, he offered to give a bit of boxing instruction after working hours in the basement. Now, I had boxed as a fifteen-year-old at the rugby club in Notting Hill and felt that I could hold my own in a friendly sparring match—how wrong I was. Eric played with me for a round or so before his straight left almost broke my nose. I felt a bit better later when I discovered from Harry that Eric had boxed very successfully for his regiment. All great characters, and it was a pleasure to have known them. One really great plus at the Board of Trade at this time was the staff canteen and restaurant. Both open to all staff, with the restaurant being waitress service at a slight increase in cost. I once took my brother-in-law, Michael Hersey, for lunch in the restaurant, and it just so happened on that day that the President of the Board of Trade, Douglas Jay, had come down to lunch with a group of his advisors. Mike, who was Chief Engineer at Telephone Rentals, was very impressed and I'm sure thought that I was a much higher grade than the lowly one I actually was. After a while, I passed the test and was promoted to the grand rank of Photo Printer 1, and after a further year or so I was successfully interviewed for the post of Assistant Chief Photo Printer at an offshoot of the Board of Trade, Export Intelligence, which was situated on the Whitechapel Road near the now-famous Brick Lane. A very interesting and cosmopolitan area in the Sixties, which I enjoyed walking around in my lunch breaks.

It wasn't long before I applied for the post of Chief Photo Printer at the Department of Employment. I must have impressed the board because, much to my surprise, I got the job, but the post was at their offices in Runcorn, Cheshire. My first impressions of Runcorn are not for publication; suffice to say that I was not greatly impressed, and that is putting it very mildly. However, the people at the Department were friendly and my new boss, Alan Tighe, was a real winner. An explosives expert in his army days, Alan was not what most of the general public think of as a civil servant, and we got on famously. Having to set up the new reprographics department from scratch, we had a lot of liaising with equipment suppliers and recruiting of staff to do, all of which was done in Alan's relaxed way, and Alan was so "relaxed" at times he could barely stand. The reps from the big printing equipment companies were only too happy to push their products over lunch or dinner and we were only too happy to expand our knowledge, but we operated under a central buying policy so had little control over what we installed. Like many of the people I have worked with over the years, Alan liked a drink and had ways of having a few whiskies during the day. His best one was to leave documents casually on his desk along with his glasses and a cigarette burning in the ashtray to give the impression that he had just slipped out to speak to one of his staff but, in reality, had walked the few hundred yards to the Halton British Legion which was open all day. I would usually get a call at about 3 p.m. to come to the Legion to discuss some aspect of our work and asked to bring the car! I would arrive at the Legion to find Alan in the middle of a game of snooker and not totally sober. He would buy me a drink and then I would drive him back to the office in East Lane. In a bid to recruit suitable staff to the new unit, we arranged meetings with the managers of local job centres to present our staffing needs. Alan would always have a bottle of good malt whisky in his briefcase to smooth the way and to ensure we got the best of what was available. This strategy worked very well; in fact, it worked so well that it left one Runcorn manager fast asleep at his desk and unable to work the next day. Despite his liking for the hard stuff, I never saw Alan incapable of doing his job. He was a great boss and I really enjoyed working with him.

It was during one of these recruiting sessions that we interviewed a young lad who had a bit of a criminal record; nothing serious, but just enough to cross him off my employment list. I would have gladly taken on someone who I thought was hoping for a fresh start but this guy didn't come across as someone in that category. However, I was overruled by Mr Tighe and was persuaded to give the lad a six-month trial, but I suspected he could be trouble and he was. Steve (not his real name) was in his early twenties and the first sign of trouble was when he started to pester a young girl of seventeen who had a disability. No sooner was this dealt with when the older ladies in the office (the FSM—Formidable Scouse Mafia) sent a delegation to my office to complain about his dreadful swearing. In consultation with the welfare officer, we jointly interviewed him and told him that his swearing was unacceptable. His response was memorable: he said, "I don't f-------g swear, do I?". Steve started to take days off for no reason and then just didn't come back, and I breathed a sigh of relief.

When the unit was up and running, I found myself in charge of some twenty members of staff. All but three were ladies, mostly from Liverpool (FSM), and most of them a bit of a handful. They were all very good workers and thoroughly nice people, but they did present me with a great many problems and complaints; "I'm not working with her, she has a body odour problem," and "Why can she go early when I can't?", etc. After a year or so, Alan Tighe offered me the chance of a further promotion to Office Manager in the reprographics office in the department's headquarters at St James's, London. In order to escape my scouse problems, I agreed to a six-month trial and so started my weekly commute to London. It didn't take long for me to realise that I had made a huge mistake; the staff in the HQ building were worse than the Runcorn lot. The office I was allocated was on the top of the building and the repro department was in the basement. One of the local staff, who was very popular with the rest, had been in line for the position, so of course I was as welcome as a butcher at a vegan convention. I started off keen enough leaving Chester, where we lived by this time, on Sunday night to be in my office by 8:30 a.m. on Monday morning and returning to Chester on Friday evening. If I thought I had been bored at the Board of Trade, this new job took me into new realms of boredom. I just had nothing to do; the local staff resented my presence to the point of cutting me out of the general day-to-day work and only using me to take the can when there was a problem. I wasn't the only one who seemed not to have enough to do. I once encountered Michael Foot in one of the corridors looking for a photocopier. As this was my department, I was able to direct him to the basement. I consider this to be the most useful thing I actually did in the time I was at HQ. I didn't seem to have anyone to answer to and so my weekly commute became shorter and shorter, catching the train on Tuesday midday and returning on Thursday afternoon. My brief return to London wasn't all bad and I had some great lunch breaks in Jermyn Street pubs and walking around some of my old stomping ground in Soho. Staying in London during this time was rather odd; I no longer knew anyone to stay with and my expenses didn't run to large hotels, so it was a serious of B&Bs until I discovered Baden-Powell House in Queen's Gate, South Kensington. A great place to stay, clean, cheap, and with a wonderful breakfast, it was also very handy for the restaurants of South Kensington for solitary meals in the evening. After just a couple of months I had had enough, although I was getting on a lot better with the HQ staff, mainly I suspect because I left them to their own devices and didn't bother them. I wasn't enjoying my time in

London and was rather lonely. It was time to get back to Cheshire.

One fellow worker worth a mention at the Runcorn Offices is George Thompson. George was a former art teacher who painted in his spare time, and on various occasions the staff had the opportunity of buying a picture from him. The biggest mistake of my life was that I never took him up on buying something because George went on to become a very well-known artist with his work fetching thousands, and, financial considerations aside, his water colours of local scenes are fantastic and his oil paintings of Venice really beautiful.

Born in Wigan, he moved to Chester when he was eleven. He studied fine art at Chester School of Art and gained an art teacher's diploma at Liverpool College of Art. Since then he has spent his time teaching painting in Chester and the Wirral. He now lives in West Kirby, overlooking the estuary of the Dee.

It was at the D of E in Runcorn that I first met my lovely wife, Linda, who was a very young clerical officer at the time. We met at the Runcorn Scout Hall while playing Badminton. Linda was a very good player and I was rubbish, so we were rarely matched to play together, however, the D of E offices had a social club with a bar and this is where we ended up after the badminton sessions. The D of E in London had an arrangement with the badminton club of the law courts and had permission to join their sessions held in the Great Hall of the Royal Courts of Justice in the Strand. Several times while we were in London we took advantage of this to play in such a magnificent setting. I'm reminded of those happy days when watching a TV programme called *Law & Order: UK* where the great hall is featured.

The Royal Courts of Justice, commonly called the law courts, house both the High Court and Court of Appeal of England and Wales. Designed by George Edmund Street and built in the 1870s, it was opened by Queen Victoria in 1882 and is one of the largest courts in Europe.

\*\*\*

# Chapter 12

## *Her Majesty's Immigration Service*

The United Kingdom Immigration Service (previously known from 1920 to 1933 as the Aliens Branch and from 1933 to 1973 as the HM Immigration Service), was the operational arm of the Home Office, Immigration and Nationality Directorate. The UK Immigration Service was, until its disbandment in 2007, responsible for the day-to-day operation of front line UK Border Controls at fifty-seven ports under the Immigration Act 1971.

I had just resumed my none-too-arduous duties in Runcorn when an internal Civil Service circular hit my desk advising that the Home Office were interviewing officers of my grade for positions in HM Immigration Service. I made a few inquiries as to the nature of the job and found that I quite liked the idea of yet another change in direction, so I applied. There followed months of silence and I had given up hope when a letter came asking me to attend an interview in London. Having attended many such interviews I knew the form and was able to read *The Telegraph* on the train going down and catch up with what was going on in the world. I must have satisfied the selection board that I wasn't completely clueless because some weeks later I was told to report to Manchester Airport. Now, I was a little bit disappointed because I had requested a posting to Heathrow. On the training course two weeks later, I met another new trainee called Dave Garlick who had been working in Manchester and had requested a posting to Manchester. Of course, the Home Office in their wisdom sent Dave to Dover and me to Manchester Airport. The training course lasted seven weeks with two of those working with a mentor at Heathrow. It was there that I was introduced to "Dodge City", otherwise known as the staff bar.

I can't say I enjoyed the training course, as learning the complicities of the 1971 Immigration Act was not my idea of a good read. However, the trainers, who were all Immigration Officers and Chief Immigration Officers, were a good bunch and very competent in what they did. Trainers and pupils bonded very well and we had many a good night out, and once again I found myself acting as tour guide on trips around the hostelries of Soho. After the seven weeks were up, I headed back to Manchester to start my new career as a still green IO.

Manchester Airport (then called Ringway Airport) was opened on 25 June 1938 and during World War II was the location of RAF Ringway, which was important in the production and repair of military aircraft and training parachutists. After World War II, it gradually expanded to include massive expansion of aprons, runways, and carparks. From 1958 to late 1962, Terminal 1 was built, which was the first of the airport's modern large terminals.

In those early days as a passenger airport it only had one Immigration Officer, a gentleman called Richard James, and one custom officer, Bill Coulson. I was told by Richard that he sometimes had less than three flights a day to deal with and obviously had a lot of time on his hands. On those occasions, he and Bill retired to the airport hotel just along from and in perfect sight of the runway. When they saw the flight about to land, the pair could walk back to the terminal with plenty of time to deal with the few arriving passengers. I hear that the new border force now staffing the airport hardly find enough time to go to the loo! How times have changed.

The purpose of an immigration officer, of course, was to process arriving, and in those days departing, passengers, to ascertain if they qualified for entry to the UK and, if not, to refuse them entry. My first such refusal was of a young Filipino lad who had come to the UK with a visa to work as a waiter. To obtain such a visa, the holder should have been on a training course and have not less than three years in the job and, critically, be over twenty-one years of age. It was easy to spot that the lad's passport had been doctored and his date of birth altered. He was in fact only seventeen years old and became my first refusal. I wouldn't like to say who was the most upset, him or me, when I saw him off on the plane, as he was in a flood of tears. The refusals became easier over the years, but I like to think that I never sent anyone home who was a genuine visitor or had a right to come to the UK. It was expected in the Seventies, but never officially spoken of, that every IO would remove a certain number of passengers each year and if not, they were not doing their job properly. As I was still in the service on retirement, I guess I had maintained my quota, but I was certainly never what was called "a knock-off king" and I always slept well at night. The majority of Immigration Officers have a lot of compassion and sympathy with a good deal of the passengers they remove or deport and are aware that a lot of them have next to nothing. With this in mind, we started a collection of clothes and shoes at Manchester, held in the detention suite, to issue to those in need. One of the saddest but funniest sights I ever saw at the airport was a Nigerian gentleman being shown to the plane on his way back to Lagos wearing a vest, flip-flops, and one of my old blue pinstriped suits, and very proud he looked too. Like the police and other emergency services, there is a lot of black humour bandied about which helped all of us do a very difficult and stressful job.

There were certain categories of deportees we were not concerned about removing from the UK. One such person was a Hong Kong national who we will call Georgie. Georgie was an enforcer for one of the Triads who operated in Manchester at the time and had to be deported more than once. A small man with an affable nature who was always smiling, but was perhaps one of the most dangerous men I have ever encountered. He was allegedly responsible for several murders and a string of mutilations; his weapon of choice was the Chinese meat cleaver and I believe that failure to pay the Triads protection could result in someone losing one or two hands. The police brought him to court many times but could never find a witness to testify, and as he was always in the country illegally, he was just deported. Along with a police escort, I once accompanied him to the British Airways check-in desk to book him in for his flight back to Hong Kong. He asked me what type of seat he had been allocated. When told that it was in economy class, he produced a huge wad of bank notes and offered to pay his own fare but in first class. I often wonder how, if indeed he is still alive, he got on under a unified China. Triad gangs are Chinese organised crime groups that have been linked to prostitution, people trafficking, drug smuggling, and extortion. The Wo, who it was alleged Georgie worked for, is largely based in Manchester and is suspected of being the most powerful Triad faction in the UK.

I could fill a whole book with the exploits and tales of some of my old colleagues but will try to stick to a few of the lighter moments. One is the tale of a lovely man called Don Collie. Don was an Anglo-Indian and as pukka as Gordon's Gin. On holiday one time in the Scottish Highlands, he was stopped by the police for speeding. Don tried to tell the old police sergeant that he was one of Her Majesty's Immigration Officers. This sometimes worked in those days to get off with a caution, however, the sergeant's response was "Oh, dear me—she's not going to be too happy with this." Don was always desperate for promotion and would joke with me that when Terminal 3 was built, we should both transfer to Heathrow where we stood a better chance of higher office. My reply was always "You go ahead and I will join you when Terminal 5 is complete." Well, Don got his wish and transferred on promotion but sadly never lived long enough to enjoy his move, and Terminal 5 is now up and running.

There are many tales of encounters between the immigration staff and travelling celebrities, but the one I found hilarious was the one between Elizabeth Taylor and an Immigration Officer:

IO: "How long do plan to stay in the UK?"

ET: "Why are you asking all these questions? Don't you know who I am?"

IO: "Madam, under all that make-up, you could be anybody!"

There are many such tales as these, but very few that can be published.

I once asked a group of my colleagues at Heathrow who they thought was the worst personality to deal with and overwhelmingly came the answer: Michael Miles, the quiz show host. Apparently, he was one of the rudest people to pass through the airport.

All immigration offices in the days before they became Border Force Barracks were filled with officers who spoke a foreign language. It was, in fact, a condition of service that you passed one exam before you became established. Manchester was no exception and we had some very accomplished linguists in a variety of languages. You were paid an allowance for speaking up to five languages, three classed as elementary (France, German, Spanish, etc.) and two classed as difficult (Russian, Arabic, Chinese, etc.) Quite a few at Manchester spoke all five but one of my old friends stands out: Chris Williams. Chris was short of one of the difficult languages, so he thought he would give Cantonese a try. He duly phoned the Home Office to get the language tapes he needed to study, only to be told that they were out for the next six months. However, the helpful young lady at the at the other end of the phone informed Chris that they had Cantonese from German tapes! Chris (who isn't German) agreed to take the tapes and unbelievably, in a very short space of time, passed the exam and was using his Cantonese in interviews. Chris is a big Yorkshire lad who smoked a pipe and was a devotee of *Coronation Street* (one of my guilty pleasures) and when we were on the same duty we would drive the rest of the office nuts, purposely I might add, in discussing Corrie's latest plot. The conversation would go something like:

"Now, our Bob, what do you think about Ken's latest shenanigans?"

"Well, Chris, I think it will all end in tears, don't you?"

And so on until someone told us to shut up in some old Anglo-Saxon language.

Lovely man is Chris; I hope he's doing well.

Another legend at Manchester was Jack Ryan, a Yorkshire man who took meanness to a new level. Jack had been in the Royal Navy during the war and had sailed on Russian convoys. He never married but seemed to have no difficulty attracting lady friends, of which he had many. This was a mystery to most of us as we all knew that Jack's favourite phrase was "Shall we go Dutch?". Older women thought he was wonderful despite his frugal approach to paying for anything and his habit of sharing his food with anyone within firing distance of his mouth. Jack had the proud boast that he had been on fifty-six cruises, but I can't recall him actually taking someone with him. He was a very accomplished painter who had been taught by an old workmate of mine, George Thompson, who is now a very well-known artist. Some months before he died aged eighty-four, I took Jack for a drink and went to see his paintings at his flat with a view of buying one. Bearing in mind that Jack had no relatives and that all his paintings would be just given to a charity shop or thrown away on his passing, you would have thought that he would be glad to receive a few pounds and have someone who knew him remember him from time to time. I selected a small watercolour of the Lake District and asked Jack how much he would take for it. His answer almost floored me; I think I could have bought an original George Thompson for the same price. As they used to say at the *News of the World*, I made my excuses and left. I liked Jack and at one time at the start of my immigration career he was asked to mentor me, and at that time we had two stamps, a square one and a triangular one. Jack's advice was "there is only one thing you need to know in this job— it's triangular for arriving passengers and square for departing passengers."

He got that wrong, as it was the other way around.

A man I really liked was a CIO called John Murrell. John came to Manchester from Heathrow with a reputation for "liking a bet" and at that time several of us were in the habit of playing a few hands of bridge during our breaks. This came to the attention of the inspector, Jeff Hopton, who called John into his office and told him that he suspected that gambling in the form of card games was going on in the office. Quick as a flash, John said, "Leave it to me, sir. I will sort it out." He returned to the office rubbing his hands and asking where the poker was being played and could he sit in. John fulfilled an ambition on his retirement to work in a betting shop chalking up and working out the odds. Sadly, that was short lived, as automatic screens came in a few months after he started. When John retired, he moved to Exeter to be with his son but, tragically, his son died in a motorcycling accident and John took his own life shortly afterwards.

One thing that always cheered the office up was the return from Paris of a private aircraft, owned and operated by a couple who ran a small charter operation. They always returned with armfuls of baguettes which they dropped off on their way through the terminal. It was a first-come-first-grab basis and the smell of warm bread wafting through the office was magical. Most of the bread was gone within minutes, either eaten there and then or stashed in desks to take home; a real touch of France on a wet afternoon in Manchester. Something else that put a smile on the office population was the return from their holidays of certain staff members. There was a tradition, quite unofficial and possibly against Home Office rules on drinking while on duty, in the Manchester Office that each IO returning from holiday would drop off a bottle of something alcoholic on his or her way home. The guidelines were that the drink had to be the national tipple of the country visited and that it had to be the cheapest alcohol one could get. It got to be very competitive in so much as we tried to produce a bottle of something that was truly disgusting and bottles of such things as ouzo, grappa, banana liqueur, retsina, and many more. It is a testament to the whole of the office for not wanting to offend their returning colleagues by leaving any of the generous gift undrunk by the following morning. However, there was one time a bottle of quite revolting grappa which was left in the office by a returning IO (you know who you are, Neil) and was still only half drunk two days later. Questions were beginning to be asked—had someone found something that was so disgusting and cheap that no one would touch it? A day later, a certain IO returned from a few days off and lo and behold, the bottle was found empty the next morning, restoring the faith in the tradition. By the time I had moved to Terminal 2, this practice had run its course, and I'm now told that alcohol is banned in all of the offices.

Part of the duties of the IO, and a part that became more and more so as the years went by, was political asylum work. In the early Seventies, those seeking asylum at Manchester were very few and far between but by the time I retired in 2002, they were a daily occurrence. I disliked this aspect of the work, not because the interviews had to be long and detailed, but because the decision of whether or not to grant asylum was out of the hands of the Immigration Service and taken by someone in the Home Office who never got to talk to the applicant and in fact was usually a grade no higher than ourselves. In the case of PA (political asylum) where it was abundantly clear that the applicant didn't have a genuine fear of returning to their own country and was most certainly an economic migrant, I would make recommendations and give an opinion, but later on we were told not to voice our own opinions but to just send a report to the Home Office where the file sat in a pile for months or even years. Over the years, I must have interviewed a great many PA applicants but can honestly say that I can count the number of what I would consider to be genuine cases in single figures. This was borne out on a couple of occasions when we spotted return passengers, having previously been granted asylum months before, coming back from a holiday in the country they had a fear of returning to. The really genuine PA applicants stood out like a sore thumb and the most obvious and high-profile case I ever dealt with was the case of a son of Canaan Banana, the first president of Zimbabwe.

The office of the President of Zimbabwe was established in 1980, when the country gained independence from the United Kingdom. Methodist minister Canaan Banana became the first president and he served until 1987 in a mostly ceremonial role. The real power was vested in the Prime Minister, Robert Mugabe. By the time I interviewed the son, Mr Banana had been imprisoned on spurious charges and his whole family were in real danger. After the interview I very quickly contacted the Home Office duty officer who took over the case, and later the whole family was granted leave to stay in the UK.

Another aspect of immigration work was seaman control, and at Manchester this meant going to Salford Docks and boarding ships that had certain foreign seaman working on board. Usually this involved Iron Curtain countries, and a lot of the time the work was carried out in collaboration with Special Branch (SB). As interesting as this work was, it was fraught with danger—the danger of getting blind drunk. The hospitality of those nations is legendary, none more so than with their seafaring men, and on entering the captain's cabin the cry was always "Welcome—we will have vodka." Not wanting to offend, the offer to toast our two nations was usually taken up, and sometimes with devastating results, like the time an IO, who will be nameless, dropped his official case containing all his stamps and a set of books containing hundreds of names of interest, into Salford Dock, and as far as I know it still remains beneath several metres of water. On one such seaman duty I had to visit a small Greek coaster that was docked at Cadishead, near Warrington. The ship was moored some distance from the road and so myself and an SB Officer set off across the railway lines in the dock area to this rusty old coaster.

Halfway there, we met a lady going in the opposite direction who could only be described as looking very rough and to be honest, past her best. The SB Officer had in the past been part of the vice squad with the Greater Manchester Police and recognised the lady as being well-known to him. He greeted her with a cheery "Hello, Mary, have you had a good night?". With a big smile on her face, she told us that she had had to service the whole crew but had earned a small fortune. Opening her purse, she showed us a couple of handfuls of Greek Drachma notes which probably amounted to less than £5. I felt extremely sorry for Mary but alas, there wasn't much we could do except give the captain and crew a thorough vetting.

The king of Salford Docks was Eric Jackson, who had been stationed in the immigration docks office for some time before being transferred to the airport when the small office inside the docks closed. Eric was known to everyone who worked in the docks, from the ships' captains and the shipping agents to the police on the gates and many of the dockers. Those who knew him well could always rely on a cup of tea and a warm by Eric's gas fire, and at Christmas, something a bit stronger than tea. Eric was an amazing man who had met and married a German girl, bringing her to the UK after the war. He cycled everywhere, including a some thirty-mile round trip each day to work. He had a lovely daughter who, at the time of Eric working at the airport, was cabin crew for British Airways, and if the end of their shifts coincided she would come into the immigration office to meet him. On these occasions, some of the younger IOs thought it only polite to go and talk to the daughter. Seeing this, Eric would move like lighting to chaperone his daughter regardless of what he was doing and never left her alone for very long.

In the Seventies and Eighties, the Immigration Service had to deal with telephone calls from MPs who tried to make representations on behalf of a relative of a constituent who was being detained or about to be deported. At Manchester, those representations usually came from North West MPs who had a large immigrant population in their constituency. In the forefront of those were the late lamented Sir Gerald Kaufman, and Jack Straw. I never crossed swords with Mr Straw, but Sir Gerald and I had a couple of "interesting" phone calls and I saw a side of him not seen by the general public—anger and a raised voice. Obviously, arguing with members of Parliament was way above my pay grade, but quite a lot of the time you would be the only one in the office. The two things to guarantee upsetting Mr Kaufman (as he was then) were pronouncing his name wrong and having to inform him that he would have to go through the Home Office to have any action stopped. There can't be many jobs where you can upset an MP but this was certainly one of them. I recall a phone conversation between an MP, can't remember who, and an Immigration Officer who shall remain nameless but is now a chiropodist living in Australia, where the discussion was becoming very heated indeed. I heard my colleague say "No, I don't know who you are. Do you know my name? No? Well, piss off," as he put the phone down. Remarkably, I can't recall a complaint being made. The Immigration Officer involved (we shall call him Scouse) was the biggest waste of talent I have ever seen; a really great linguist with an acting talent that could have put him in any West End production. He was in an Amateur Dramatics group that put on productions at the Garrick Theatre in Stockport, and I saw him playing the recruiting sergeant in a production of *Oh! What a Lovely War*. In a very good cast, Scouse stood out. He could have quite easily turned professional.

I have no wish to upset my Liverpudlian friends, but Scouse did come from that great city and unfortunately also suffered from the characteristic that certain residents are portrayed to have. I liked Scouse, and one New Year's Eve we were asked to a party at his house. Linda, who was a civil servant at the time, noticed a very nice wall clock and said to the surrounding company, "I have one just like that in my office." Of course, the clock was government issue and had gone missing from someone else's office. Scouse's downfall came several years later over an incident in the Manchester office. Scouse was on night duty one evening and during the night his partner for the night, who was in a different room, heard banging coming from the main office, and thinking it was some form of work being carried out by the airport staff, ignored it. The next day, Dave Pemberton was at his desk in the main office when he went to lower the window blind and found that it was missing. The inspector was informed and a delegation of police and a CIO went around to Scouse's address and, lo and behold, found the missing blind. Scouse was charged and at his appearance in the magistrates' court put on such a performance (someone from the office who was in court described it as being better than Lord Olivier could have given) that he was given a suspended sentence. He was allowed to resign, but the sad part of this sorry tale is that the blind was too big and didn't fit.

The Christmas parties at the airport were legendary. Every office and department held a festive do, from a small travel agency called Star Travel who served sherry and mince pies in the afternoon to the Special Branch party that went on until the small hours. It's unthinkable now, but all these functions were held in the various offices, a lot of which were airside, and alcohol was freely available. The Immigration Christmas party was acknowledged to be one of the best. An ex-colleague, who had left the IS to join the police service on the Isle of Man, came over with a barrel of real ale which was set up in our rest room and the clerical staff, Betty and the lovely Norma, prepared the food. From time to time we had a few well-known faces attend our Christmas festivities. We were living very close to Steve Coppell, the Manchester United and England footballer, and his wife Jane. We became friends, and one year, Steve and another friend, Ian Chadwick, came to the office party. Needless to say, Steve was a great attraction and we seemed to have a lot more female airline staff attend that year. Another famous face that showed up one year was Hurricane Higgins, the snooker world champion, who was brought along by a member of Special Branch, Ray Cronie. After a very short time at the party, Higgins asked Ray, for no apparent reason, to take him home. He went into his house and came out a few minutes later wearing a different shirt and asked Ray to take him back to the party. Apparently, he had gone wearing the wrong shirt. Brilliant snooker player but a bit eccentric.

Over the years working at Manchester Airport I always volunteered to work on Christmas Day. It gave those in the office with children a chance to be home on Christmas Day, and it meant that I didn't have to go into the draw to work on New Year's Eve, a special time for my Scottish wife. In the late Seventies, Christmas Day at the airport was a very quiet affair with only two or three flights, but the office had to be almost fully staffed in case of one of the other airports in the country being closed due to bad weather and all their flights diverted to Manchester. Failing that horrible scenario, Christmas Day at Manchester was a chance to catch up and take things easy. However, I recall that one Christmas Day, I managed to refuse entry to three passengers who were inadmissible—a personal record. One of the nice touches to happen was that after the morning flights arrived, British Airways always laid on lunch for their staff working on the day, and we were always invited.

During the summer months, the Immigration Service took on a small group of seasonal officers to help out with the summer increase in passenger numbers. These were always retired gentlemen who had previously been in positions of some standing. Among the group that returned each year were a bank manager, a senior manager with British Aircraft Manufacturers, a top civil servant, and, one year, a chief superintendent of police. These gentlemen were welcomed each year with open arms as they took over the job of checking the passports of embarking passengers— their only function, and one which full time IOs disliked. A lovely man called Wilf Reilly was one such seasonal IO. An ex-bank manager and secretary of one of the top golf clubs in Cheshire, he once asked me if I could relieve him on the embarkation desk as he had been told his car was blocking someone in. While I waited for Wilf's return, a Special Branch Officer came over to chat and asked me if Wilf had moved his white convertible Rolls Royce yet. I thought he was joking, but no, this was the car Wilf used every day.

Dear old Wilf. When he passed on, I attended his funeral. It was the very first one that I had ever been to. Unhappily, it was the first of many, some very sad affairs, others a cerebration of the deceased's life, and one or two very weird. The best, if one can describe any funeral as "best", was a good friend who lived on Delamere Park. Derek Wynne was a lecturer in law at Manchester University who in his fifties was playing football with a local amateur team when he went up to head the ball and was dead before he hit the ground. Derek's funeral was extremely well attended with mourners from the university, Delamere Park, and many friends. There were many eulogies with a great number of stories about Derek's life which contained a lot of humour and, knowing him, it would have been just what he would have wanted. The most unusual funeral I ever attended was for a friend of my wife's who had worked with her, and it was a humanist service. John had a very good voice and had made several tapes of himself singing, which were played during the ceremony. His wicker coffin was festooned with photographs of him with family and friends, and the congregation were encouraged to get up close and take a look. Not wanting to give offence, I had a little look and nearly fainted when I saw a photo of myself pinned to the side of the coffin. Although he was a very good friend of my wife's, I had only met John a couple of times, but on one of those occasions a photo had been taken, and there I was for all to see. More of my own last wishes later!

The real legend of the SIO's was undoubtedly Terry Cochran, the civil servant. Terry had been a senior principal in the Home Office and even after retiring was called upon from time to time to do the odd job for them. On these occasions, he disappeared for a few days but never talked about what he had been up to, and we never asked. He was the most immaculate dresser, always in a well-tailored suit, white shirt, and silk handkerchief in his top pocket. Terry was always in for his shift a good hour early, and on an early duty this was a godsend for the regular staff on night duty as they had to cover the embarkation desk from 5 a.m., and the SIO didn't start until 6 a.m. The night duties at Manchester were taken as a double shift, from 6 p.m. to 8 a.m. the next morning, and because of the long hours, a day bed was provided to rest in between long gaps in flights. On many occasions when I had been resting prior to opening the embarkation desk, a knock on the door of the rest room would be followed by Terry handing me a cup of tea and telling me not to get up as he had Embarks covered. A wonderful man, and much missed when the government stopped checks on departure.

We always had to bring our own food on nights, and of all the meals produced on night duties, two names stand out: Stuart Horner and Claire Howarth. Stuart went to evening classes to learn Indian cookery and produced the most fantastic meals. He ground all his own spices, the secret of great Indian dishes, and came up with the best curries I have ever had. Claire was just a fantastic cook; she produced meals with a different nationality theme and one of her best was a Scandinavian meal complete with aquavit to match the food. Other colleagues cooked or brought meals in, and I like to think that I myself came up with some enjoyable dishes in my time. There was no staff canteen and working a double night shift required everyone to bring in some form of food. A lot of us at Manchester just went that bit more upmarket.

Unless one has a rather black sense of humour, you may not find the following two tales of airport life very funny, but they nevertheless happened. One of my colleagues, who shall remain nameless, was on the embarkation control one afternoon when a porter came through with an elderly Asian lady in a wheelchair. The lady appeared to be fast asleep and, not wanting to wake her, as all her travel documents were in order, waved her through the control. When the airline staff tried to get her into her seat they found, to their horror, that in fact the lady was dead and had been for several days. It transpired that the son had bought her ticket to go home some weeks before but she had expired two days before the flight, and he claimed that he was unable to get a refund on the ticket so was merely using the ticket he had paid for.

Equally bizarre was the time that British Airways check-in staff became rather suspicious of a gentleman who was trying to check in a very large and heavy trunk. Fearing that foul play had taken place and, horror of horrors, a body was in the trunk, they phoned Special Branch to urgently attend. They were spot on; his wife's body was in the trunk but she was alive, and he was sending her home by freight as it was considerably cheaper than a passenger ticket. I never found out if he was prosecuted or not, but that airline girl saved the wife's life.

The Immigration Service, along with the rest of the Civil Service, had a unique way of dealing with staff who, for reasons of severe weather or transport strikes, etc., were unable to attend their normal place of work. In those circumstances, staff were required to report to their nearest government building. I had occasion to follow this procedure once when visiting in-laws in Aberdeen over Christmas. I was snowed in when the airport was closed on New Year's Day, and I was a due to fly back for a 3:30 p.m. shift. It being a bank holiday, I was loath to lose the double time shift pay for that day, so reported to the nearest government establishment which was in fact Aberdeen Airport. My brother-in-law Robert, who couldn't believe what I was doing, drove me to the airport, and I wasn't very surprised to hear that all the Scottish IOs I knew were on leave. I was made welcome by the two English guys on duty, but horrified to be told that my presence was most fortuitous as they were joining the police later that morning for a raid on some premises in the city and that I could help with that. I was mightily relieved when they took a phone call to say that the police were unable to accompany them on the planned raid and I could stay in the warmth of the office for the day. The best part of that day was catching up with an old friend in HM Customs, Jim Innes, who had been at Manchester Airport and who I had played five-a-side football with on many occasions. When my brother-in-law Robert picked me up later in the day, he wouldn't believe that I would be paid for my visit to Aberdeen Airport.

In the course of a working day we tended to work very closely with our colleagues in HM Customs and Excise. Today both forces have combined to form the Border Force and, like ourselves, their service threw up its share of characters. One such character was Jack Prest, a huge man whose means of transport was an old ambulance, and his claim to fame was that he had once stopped one of the royal's protection officers trying to smuggle a suitcase full of cigarettes. One day, Jack stopped an MP, who shall be nameless, and in the course of the bag search the MP, who was Jewish, accused Jack of being anti-Semitic and threatened to complain. After the MP left the airport, Jack made a few enquires and, on the next Sabbath, complete with yarmulke, turned up at the MP's synagogue and again introduced himself to the MP. Jack, of course, was Jewish. There was no complaint.

If we wanted to search a passenger's luggage, as we had the power to do so, we would always enlist the help of a customs officer because if drugs were found it was far more straightforward when it came to the prosecution. One day I questioned a Nigerian gentleman and needed to search his bags. When the customs officer I had asked to carry out the search opened his case we found four giant, and I mean gigantic, snails. The giant West African snail (*Archachatina marginata*) can grow up to twenty centimetres long and live up to ten years.

The snails had had a hole punched through their shells and were strung together with a piece of rope. The guy explained that they were a present for the person he was coming to visit and they intended to have the tasty molluscs for dinner. The snails had travelled in the aircraft hold and we naturally thought that they were dead, but as they warmed up in the heat of the customs area, and much to our horror, they started to move about. The passenger's documents and visa were in order, so I was content to grant his two-month visit and very relieved to hand the problem of the snails to my rather unhappy friend from customs. I later learned that there had been much discussion with the Environmental Health Department and other agencies, and in the end the passenger was allowed to take his dinner away but had to promise that the snails would be destroyed humanely! As one of my more philosophic colleagues, Ernie Briscoe, was prone to say, "What a daft job."

A gentleman I must write about is a certain Jagdash Chadda, who for many years in the department was one of our interpreters and indeed, at the time of writing, still was. Jag is of Indian descent but was born and raised in Kenya, and before coming to the UK worked for the Kenyan Customs Service. His first job in the UK was as a security officer at Manchester Airport, which is where I first encountered him. Jag claimed to speak three Asian languages plus Swahili, and so he was taken on as one of our interpreters, and what an interpreter he turned out to be. He was not like the other interpreters who purely translated word for word. Jag gave his opinion in no uncertain terms and would utter the word "dodge" quite early in the interview. Surprisingly enough, he was inevitably right in a lot of cases, but we only found this out after hours of tedious questions and many enquiries. In one infamous case, Jag was interpreting when the IO interviewing decided that the man being questioned was telling a pack of lies and that a caution was required. He asked Jag to translate the usual "You are not obliged to say anything", etc., but according to the man's solicitor, Jag allegedly translated this as: "If you don't tell the officer the

118

truth, I'm going to break both your legs." This was vehemently denied by Jag and no further action was taken, but I'm sure the requests to use Jag in preference to the other interpreters doubled. Because Jag has worked in this role for over thirty years, he is obviously very well-known in the Indian restaurants and shops of Greater Manchester, and I am amazed by the number of people he seems to know. In restaurants, he never tips and always seems to get a large discount on the bill. I have known him to return to the restaurant when hearing we had left a tip to retrieve it. One tale of Jag is like something out of a Liverpool comedy. Jag's mother-in-law passed away and in keeping with her wishes to have her ashes scattered on the sea, the task was handed to Jag, who thought, "Southport is the nearest stretch of sea; we will go there." The family piled into cars and set off for Southport, but had neglected to check the tides, and this is one of the largest tidal waters in the UK with the sea going out some two miles from the land, and this was one of those times where the sea was out of sight. Jag's next idea was, "Liverpool has an opening to the sea. We'll do it there." The family arrived in Liverpool and Jag suggested that they catch the ferry and scatter the remains of Mum-in-law from the ferry. This may be a regular occurrence as the captain very kindly stopped the boat for a few moments while the ashes went overboard. Jag told me the next day that they all seemed happy with his arrangements and everyone had a good day. Having some great memories of times spent in that city, I may request the same treatment myself, organised of course by Mr Chadda. I have remained good friends with Jag and his wife Pritiba and have had many a great curry with them.

The very best working time at Manchester Airport was when I was selected to be part of a small team of five to set up the immigration office and controls that would be needed at the future Terminal 2. The team consisted of Manisha Kotecha, Jackie Jarvis, Derek Howcroft, and myself under the leadership of CIO Nick Boston. We had some four months to liaise with the airport authorities in setting up the control and watch house (a small office behind the arrival desks) and the main office where we had to buy all the furniture, etc. This really was the very best of times; we had no set hours to work to and had many excursions to shops and department stores to buy furniture and office supplies. It was completely left to ourselves and the home office even gave us a credit card to pay for it all. Even if I say this myself, we made a damned good job of it and the main office looked superb.

It was quite an eye-opener to see the terminal taking shape and it was brilliant to be a very small part of that. On opening day, the Queen, who was due to cut the ribbon, was unfortunately unwell and the Duke of Edinburgh had to stand in. As you can imagine, the ceremony and lunch to follow was magnificent and much appreciated by the four of us who attended. After that it rather went downhill when the first passengers started to use the terminal a few weeks later, but I will never forget those few months.

The inspector stationed at Manchester Airport was also responsible for the Liverpool district, including the airport at Speke, now the John Lennon Airport. At times of staff shortages in the Liverpool city office, who sent officers to Speke when flights were due and to cover diversions from Manchester in fog, etc., we were given the job of covering the airport. People who fly from Liverpool Airport today could never imagine the old building and the state of the immigration premises. Our office and the baggage reclaim area were housed in an old hanger which was home to a population of pigeons and the odd rat. It had no heating;

the office had a small electric fire and I can't recall ever not catching a cold after a short spell working there. Diversions were a nightmare as the airport was not equipped to handle large numbers of passengers and if by chance you had to detain someone, the unfortunate person spent a night in the old bridewell, which usually resulted in the detainee asking, if not begging, to be sent home. All Liverpool Police Stations with cells were called "bridewells", and the main bridewell was classified as a prison with a police chief inspector as the governor. Everyone entering saw a plaque on the wall which read, "Please do not ask for bail because a refusal often offends"—that old black humour again. The main bridewell finally closed as a prison in 1999 and is now a hotel which I have never been tempted to stay at.

Over the years I worked in the Immigration Service, I met a lot of famous and well-known people. Many IOs, mainly at Heathrow, kept autograph books, and as you can imagine had a very large collection of celebrity autographs at the end of their service. One of the most charismatic and quite one of the nicest men I ever had the pleasure of talking to was Omar Sharif. This lovely man seemed extremely modest and despite the fact that he could have lived in and obtained US citizenship, still travelled on an Egyptian passport with all the visa requirements that entailed. I once had an interesting conversation with him after I asked him if he still played bridge. He said, "Not so much; my interest lies with horses these days."

"Well, I've seen Lawrence of Arabia, so I know you are a good rider."

"No, dear boy, it's racing I'm interested in, and you shouldn't believe everything you see on the screen. I wasn't that good."

I couldn't believe it when the Service Air girl escorting him came to me afterwards and asked who he was. I spoke to him a few times over the years and he was always the perfect gentleman, a truly great star who is sadly missed. Not every personality was as nice as Omar Sharif. A certain singer comes to mind, who I won't name but allegedly has a girlfriend who possibly lives at the "top of the town". On the embarkation desk one morning, a young lady from the ground staff, Service Air, came up to me and said that this individual was about to come through the controls and would I get his autograph for her. Well, he refused point blank to sign her book, saying he didn't have time, and I know I shouldn't have but I was so incensed I made him fill an embarkation card of which I cut off the signature and gave it to a very happy young lady. Working on the arrivals desk one evening I was distracted by my colleague, a young British Pakistani girl, who said to her passenger, "Well, what sort of musician are you?". I heard him reply, "Well, I play the piano and sing a bit," to which she said, "Well, I've never heard of you." At this point, I felt I had to intervene and leaned over to her desk and introduced her to Fats Domino. To defuse any possible complaint, I said to Fats, "Sorry, she's very young, and I don't suppose that you have ever heard of Ravi Shankar." There was no complaint. I was sad to hear, while putting the finishing touches to my book, that Fats Domino had passed away on 24 October 2017 at the age of eighty-seven.

Another visitor to these shores who was always very pleasant to talk to was the legendary rock star Alice Cooper. Born Vincent Damon Furnier, Alice Cooper was the name of his first group, which he later adopted as his own, and he was one of the nicest people you could wish to meet. He was always prepared to have a short chat but not as you would expect about music, no—golf. Quite a different character to pass through the airport on a couple of occasions was the great ballet star Rudolf Nureyev. He was never talkative and always maintained an air of mystery, striding along in a large hat and black cloak. He was perhaps the most impressive person I have ever seen.

My big claim to fame came the morning I issued James Brown with a notice detaining him for further questioning. On night duty one evening with Dave McDonough, I took a phone call from the Home Office duty officer who informed me that he had just been contacted by Interpol, who in turn had received information from the New York police. They claimed that James Brown had earlier that evening been involved in a fatal shooting in the city and was now on his way to Manchester on the red eye special. Mr Brown duly arrived in the early hours of the morning together with some of his band and a very slick young lawyer who spoke for James. He told me that it was all a big mistake and that a witness had mistaken James for someone else. Mr Brown himself seemed to be very jetlagged and didn't seem to know what was going on. He was getting rather old by then. By the time we confirmed with the Home Office duty officer that we had Mr Brown detained, it was time to hand the case to one of the day staff and go home. I learnt the following day that Mr Brown had been granted leave to enter the UK for two months to perform at his concerts and as nothing was heard of him being charged on his return to the USA, I presume that it had all been the mistake it was claimed to be, but the thought that I may have been involved in a James Brown murder inquiry had made for an exciting night duty. Dave later left the service and went on to become an analyst at Liverpool FC and Valencia before taking up the post of Director of Technical Performance and Scouting with West Bromwich Albion.

Immigration officers were obliged to write reports on almost everything they did but the most dreaded report was the "I regret" one. This had to be submitted to the chief inspector if one became a subject of a complaint or their actions embarrassed the service. Luckily, I had very few to write, but the most crawling one came as a consequence of me pulling out of a posting to India at the last minute. I had applied for and been selected to fill the post of entry certificate officer with the diplomatic service in New Delhi, India. The pay and allowances were fine, and I was looking forward to seeing the country, the only place of which I had been before was Bombay (now Mumbai). With just a couple of weeks to go before my departure, the Foreign Office stopped all allowances for staff seconded on a temporary basis and replaced them with a top-up on your UK salary. The Foreign Office allowances covered various domestic expenses while abroad and without them I would have not been able to pay for my mortgage, etc., at home. When I phoned the deputy chief inspector to explain and withdraw my application, he was, shall we say, not best pleased and I had not heard language coming out of the other end of the phone like that since my Merchant Navy days. Needless to say, my "I regret" report to the Foreign Office was a masterpiece in crawling.

For a while, my face at the airport was recognised by quite a few arriving passengers from the USA. One day, the station manager of American Airlines came to see me and asked if I could help him with a little problem he had. The airline had upgraded me a couple of times, so I felt obliged to help him out. He wanted me to stand behind the arrival desk and be filmed processing an arriving passenger. This was to be part of a "Welcome to Manchester Airport" short instruction video showing what to do and where to go, etc. The video was to be screened just before the plane touched down into Manchester. I duly gave my best Cary Grant impression and thought no more about it until American passengers started to recognise me with, "You're the guy from the film," and "Hey, I've just seen you on the plane." After a few months of this, and never having seen my performance, I quite naturally wanted to see how I had done. So, one day when I bumped into the station manager, I asked him if it would be possible to view the video, thinking from a seat in the first-class cabin on my way to Los Angeles. Alas, he arranged for me to be shown the video when the aircraft was being cleaned prior to departing! Sometime later the recognition stopped and I suppose they found a more photogenic star.

This wasn't the only time I appeared on film. One afternoon I was asked to attend a small aircraft that was just about to land for a tarmac clearance. When I got to the plane, there seemed to be a lot of photographers around, so not wanting to speak to the passengers in full view of the cameras, I got onto the aircraft. They were all well-known golfers coming to play in the British Open at Royal Birkdale, and among the recognisable faces was Bernhard Langer. I did the necessary and got out of the plane just ahead of Mr Langer and thought no more about it until that evening watching the BBC news. There I was, as bold as brass—a friend of Bernard's or a professional golfer?

When I think of writing reports and statements, two Manchester colleagues spring to mind—Dave Fuller and Neil Rowland. Dave is a man who never used one word when fifty would do, and Neil was known for his colourful descriptions that had completely no relevance to the subject matter. In fact, he was known as "It-was-a-dark-and-stormy-night Rowland". Neil is one of my oldest friends; I was an usher at his wedding to Heather. We have had some great times together and I hope he doesn't mind me mentioning his descriptive writing.

A great character who sadly passed away as I was writing this chapter was Eric Wilkinson. Eric was a great military enthusiast who collected army uniforms, and although there are many tales of Eric during his Heathrow days, two come to mind. He wanted to display one of the uniforms in his collection and to this end bought, unseen, a tailor's dummy. Unfortunately, the goods turned out to be a female model, but much to the hilarity of his flatmates, he went ahead and put the uniform on display and this was perhaps the first time a guard's officer (this was in the Seventies) became a woman. During troop movements, we occasionally had regiments passing through Manchester Airport and Eric, always keen to chat to the officers in charge, engaged the CO of this particular Scottish regiment in conversation. He was heard to tell the CO that he had a number of regimental uniforms himself and in a distinct Edinburgh Morningside accent, the officer replied, "My, what a chequered career you must have had." Eric left the Immigration Service before retirement, eventually taking up a job as an archivist at Lancaster Castle and becoming a magistrate. Given his rather right-wing views, his old colleagues expected to hear that the first life sentence for speeding had been passed down in Lancaster. They don't make them like Eric anymore; a real character.

When I joined the Immigration Service, if you wanted to join a trade union, you didn't have much choice but to go with the Civil & Public Services Association (CPSA). I and a lot of my colleagues felt that this union didn't represent the interests of the small number of immigration staff, and we certainly didn't agree with a lot of their policies on strikes, etc. A group of IOs and CIOs (the representative from Manchester was a nice guy but fierce negotiator called Peter Stowe) got together and formed our own union—The Immigration Service Union (ISU). The new union gained recognition from the TUC and the Home Office and, after a slow start, gradually grew into the fine association it is today. Peter remained an official of the ISU until his retirement and I'm proud to say that I was among the first to join and am now a life member.

I think probably the majority of immigration staff, after they had retired, thought that they were just forgotten, abandoned by the Home Office, and no longer existed. This prompted some of the senior officers to form an organisation for retirees and serving staff to stay in touch and to record and relive some memories. Naturally, they called it "Exist". They, or I should say we, as I am indeed a member, started with a small number of members and now have hundreds with a very active website (sorry, it's private). It's ironic that the Home Office contacted the organisers a few years ago to ask if they could possibly ask their retired members if they would like to apply for some overseas posts with the Foreign Office. Now, each year Exist get the call to trawl for an ever-increasing number of posts both in the UK and abroad. Some time ago, I made the huge mistake of telling my wife about this "opportunity", and she immediately saw golden beaches, embassy parties, and free holidays. I had to sit her down and explain that the beaches in places like Mogadishu were not that great.

The Immigration Service, being a relatively small department, has always thought of themselves as the forgotten force, always overshadowed by HM Customs and Excise. In fact, if you told the majority of the general public who you worked for, they would immediately think of searching luggage and seizing drugs. Now that the two forces have combined, a few retired guys approached the Maritime Museum in Liverpool in an attempt to highlight the work of the Immigration Service. One of the driving forces behind this quest for recognition of the Immigration Service was Pete Lacey, an IO from the Liverpool office. Thanks to him and a few others, there is a small exhibit in the Border Force National Museum collection that is on display in the customs gallery, with some very informative videos starring Mr Lacey in the work of HMIS. I myself contributed some old records and circulars as well as a few photographs, but as of yet they have not appeared on display. Another of the exhibits not yet on display is the landing card completed by Albert Einstein when he arrived at Dover on 26 May 1933 from Belgium. He states his occupation as professor and nationality as Swiss.

When I pass through Manchester or Liverpool Airports now, I don't recognise a single officer. My friends tell me that the black uniforms they now wear are very intimidating and scary and I'm glad that I never had to wear one. When I joined HM Immigration Service in 1975 it was one of the best in the world and a privilege to work in it. Sadly, one can't say the same today.

*Me looking a bit nervous as the engineers test the distance the aircraft had to come to link up with the air bridge—a bit scary when it first happened.*

\*\*\*

# Chapter 13

## *Lagos—Dreadful Place but Great Social Life*

In 1981, I applied for and was accepted for a short-term posting with the Foreign Office, thinking Paris, New York, or somewhere warm and sunny in the Caribbean. Well, I got warm, or rather hot, but it was a four-month posting to Lagos, not the first place you think of for warm seas and white sandy beaches. In fact, the main beach in Lagos, Bar Beach, had only recently stopped having public executions in the sand. In September 1971, seven armed robbers had been shot by an army firing squad and it was reported that thirty thousand spectators were on the beach to witness the executions. I was the first of three IOs to be posted to the British High Commission, which in the Eighties was on Victoria Island. My fellow Entry Certificate Officers (ECOs) were Bob Barber and Steve Watkins, who joined me two weeks after I had arrived. The three of us joined the two long-term ECOs, Dave Roy and Alp Mehmet. Alp went on to transfer from the Immigration Service to the Diplomatic Service, where he went on to become HM Ambassador to Iceland. Of Turkish-Cypriot origins, born in London, he was one of the first ethnic minority ambassadors to be appointed. Alp has now retired from the F&CO and at the time of writing is the Vice Chair of Migration Watch UK.

On my journey out to Nigeria, I flew on the Dutch airline KLM via Amsterdam, where I took advantage of a few days stopover and the hospitality of my Dutch colleagues. The Dutch Immigration and Naturalisation Service is a branch of the Dutch Ministry of Security and Justice, which implements the immigration policy of the Netherlands, and the Royal Marechaussee is responsible for border control in the Netherlands at all airports and most sea ports. The British Immigration Service had a close working relationship with the Marechaussee and we often met up, playing football against them both in Holland and in the UK. John Murrell, one of the CIOs at Manchester who had previously worked at Heathrow and had a number of contacts at Schiphol Airport, kindly arranged for me to be met and "looked after" when I arrived, and I was taken to their canteen for a meal before being driven to the hotel they had booked for me. On the drive, we witnessed a car accident just in front of us, and my two Dutch colleagues said that they would have to help while waiting for the traffic police to arrive. They both left me in the car but five minutes later came back to ask me if I could direct the traffic around the accident. I duly started to wave the cars on when one stopped and asked a question. Of course, I don't speak the language and answered in English, "I'm sorry, I don't speak Dutch." The look on the man's face spoke volumes and I would bet good money on his conversation to his passenger on the lines, "What is this country coming to when our policemen can't speak Dutch?". Four months later, I was back in Amsterdam staying at the Krasnapolsky in Dam Square where my wife had joined me for a few days R&R. One afternoon, we were having a drink in the bar when a gentleman at the next table asked the waiter something in Dutch and, lo and behold, the waiter replied in English, "I'm sorry, I don't speak Dutch." I would have loved it if it had been the same man I had encountered at that accident four months earlier. I had met my wife at the airport when she flew in to Amsterdam and through my connections with the Marechaussee, I was able to go to the arrival gate to meet her. She looked as lovely as ever as she stepped from the plane but seemed a little unsteady on her feet. In fact, she was pie-eyed. This was explained as the fault of a friend of ours, Tony Tyman, who was the catering manager for British Airways and had arranged an upgrade and a steady supply of champagne during the flight, and so after four months of not seeing my wife, I spent the first night of our reunion watching her sleeping it off.

In the early Eighties, Lagos was classed by the Foreign Office as a hardship posting, and the expenses reflected that in the form of higher allowances. Part of those allowances went on the employment of a steward to take care of the day-to-day domestic chores. I was very lucky in this, having been introduced to Joseph, a Cameroonian who was a quiet man and a really efficient steward as well as being a good cook. The amount of money we paid the local domestic staff was set in stone and the Foreign Office went to some lengths to advise the rest of us not to pay any more than the laid down rates. Most, if not all, of the domestic employees had their families with them and more important than the wages they got was any accommodation they could be given. For the High Commission staff of my lowly grade, that meant a garage at the rear of the apartments. This sounds awful but the garages all had electricity and water and if you compare this with the dreadful huts without facilities they normally had to rent, and that the garages came free, you can begin to understand. Unfortunately, I couldn't offer Joseph this facility as my garage was already occupied by the family of another diplomat's staff. After a couple of months, Joseph left my employ to go and work for a Nigerian doctor who had offered more money but before he left, he found me a replacement.

Ayodele was a completely different kettle of fish. Coming from Lagos, he was from the Yoruba ethnic group and was perhaps the most surly and ill-tempered man I have ever met, but as I only had two months to go I decided to put up with him.

After another month, Joseph turned up again and told me that the doctor had been beating him and he had left his employment. I don't know how it was arranged between the two but the next day Joseph resumed his duties, much to my relief. Joseph was a very good cook and as the main shopping area had very few food shops, if any, I was quite happy for Joseph to shop for food at the local stalls for me. Now and then a fish merchant appeared and sold boxes of huge prawns for the princely sum of about £25. Joseph was under instruction to buy a box on the man's next visit and he said he would make a seafood pie. A beautiful pie appeared for dinner the next day, but it was big enough to feed at least ten people. Given the heat and the unreliable electricity supply in Lagos, it was clear that the pie would only be half-eaten before I had to throw the remainder out. Of course, I told Joseph to take the rest for his family and I swear there was a very slight smile on his face as he took it away. One of the things we had to pay for was telephone calls we made from our apartments, and charges to and from Nigeria didn't come cheap. I came home one evening to find Joseph talking to someone on the phone. He was having a nice long chat to Linda, and after I was handed the phone she said, "He seems nice; I've had a long conversation with him and he couldn't believe that we have no children!"

After pointing out the cost of such chats, I thought no more about it, but when I finally left Lagos, Joseph gave me a straw bag for Linda and it had a large fertility emblem on the front. Sorry, Joseph, but it didn't work.

A way of life in Lagos was dash or bribes for everything. It seemed like everyone was on the take and it could make life very difficult. Full time Foreign Office staff and long-term postings from other departments were allowed to have their cars or to buy a new car and have it shipped over. When the vehicles arrived, they were kept in the customs pound and it took forever and a great deal of red tape to have them released, but if you said the magic word "dash", the cars were ready for collection. The Diplomatic Service naturally frowned on "back-handers", so our cars tended to stay off the road that bit longer. I was only twice in the position where dash was expected. When I had first arrived in Lagos, a lovely young lady called Ann had also just been posted and was one of the High Commissioner's secretaries. We had become friends, and Ann, who had her own car, kindly gave me lifts to the various functions, etc. On this occasion, we were driving home late one night when we drove through a checkpoint without stopping. Luckily, we were not going very fast and as I realised what had happened, I told Ann to stop just as the soldier on duty had raised his rifle. We reversed back and I got out of the car. I could almost read the soldiers mind, "Ah, two white people. I can demand a great deal of dash." Unfortunately for him, I had had a fair amount to drink and boosted by this, I proceeded to harangue him for stopping a car with diplomatic plates and threatened to report him to his general (go big, I always say). With the best rifle salute I have ever seen, we drove away. The next morning, I realised what I had done and was almost sick; Lagos was a dangerous place in the Eighties. The other time I avoided paying dash was when I was leaving Lagos and the security guard tried to search my bags far too thoroughly. Being in the diplomatic channel, he had no right to search the bags of departing diplomatic passport holders. I pointed this out in no uncertain times and was rewarded with another smart salute.

One of the "perks" granted to the ECOs from time to time was to take the diplomatic bag to the offices in other parts of the country. I was asked to perform this much sought-after task on one occasion and take the bag to my fellow ECO in Abuja. The Foreign Office is extremely good at making arrangements and I found myself sitting in the first-class lounge at the airport with two first-class tickets to Abuja. As the bag I was escorting was quite large and could not leave my sight, it required a seat next to me. The lounge was occupied by five or six other travellers, all Nigerian business men in traditional dress. Fifteen minutes before the flight was due to take off, we were asked to board the small twin prop aircraft some fifty yards from the lounge and were escorted, passing an alarmingly large queue of people waiting to join the same flight! I found my seats and was just beginning to relax a bit when our fellow travellers came aboard. An England versus Scotland rugby scrum had nothing on these guys. The diplomatic bag was unceremoniously dumped on the floor and the largest lady on the flight proceeded to take its seat. No amount of explaining to the lady, and with no help from the cabin staff, could shift her, and I had to content myself in keeping the bag between my legs for the whole flight—the joys of flying Air Nigeria.

During one of the national holidays when the visa section of the British High Commission was closed, the three of us were offered the chance to drive to one of the outlying posts which was no longer operating but was maintained for strategic reasons (no, I never found out why). After a long drive, we came to this lovely old building which at one time had been part of the High Commission. Inside it was like

134

the Marie Celeste of offices which had all been maintained as if still functional. A couple of locals were employed to look after the place and cook, etc., for any visitors. After having a meal of our own brought in (food, sorry to say, but Nigerian cuisine is not to Western tastes), we spent a nice night exploring the old building and it all made for a welcome break. We became friends with, let's call him, James, from the British Council who was the sole representative in Lagos and, not being part of the diplomatic community, was rather left out of things. However, he was a lovely man about our own age and it was nice to go around with him. One time we were all having a few of the deadly Nigerian beers, Star Lager, at the Embassy Court hotel when he suggested that we have a weekend across the border in Benin where you could get some decent seafood. Being the only one with his own car, he agreed to drive the few hours to the border and arrange the hotel accommodation. We set off to the border on the road to Cotonou and nearly turned back when we saw the queue of cars waiting to cross. It stretched for a mile or more, but James said that as the holders of diplomat passports, we were allowed to bypass the queue, which we did without much hassle. I recall that we stayed in a small but comfortable hotel, and as the official language is French, the touches in the hotel were very French. The atmosphere in Benin was so different from Lagos: calm, non-threatening, and a pleasure to experience. We had a great fish dinner and it was one of the best memories of the whole four months. The food on our next little trip with James wasn't so memorable. He had been invited to lunch at the University of Lagos and asked if we would like to go along. The university is situated in the suburb of Yaba, and after a short tour of the university we were taken to the lecturers' dining room for lunch. I reiterate my comments about

135

Nigerian cuisine being not to European taste; the food was terrible. The worst taste, the hottest, the sharpest, and, I'd guess, the toughest chicken imaginable, and we had to eat some out of courtesy. There is always a price to pay for a free lunch.

For diplomats and expats alike, there wasn't a great deal of things to do outside their own communities, so they formed and joined clubs, and the foremost and oldest one in Lagos was The Ikoyi Golf Club. In September 1938, the Ikoyi Club 1938 officially came into being through the merger of the European Club and Lagos Golf Club. For many years, it was essentially an expatriate's club run by top European civil servants and members of the business communities. Although hugely expensive, it offered everything you could wish for in a club: large swimming pool, tennis courts, bars, and restaurants, and of course a golf course. Well, the allowances for Nigeria were among the highest being paid so I thought, "Why not?". There wasn't much else to spend your money on, so I took out a temporary membership. It was nice to be able to go for a beer and a swim after work and I even managed to play some tennis and a few rounds of golf. Playing golf at the Ikoyi had a few "rules" you don't find in the UK. You always had a caddie who was a young lad of about fifteen to seventeen years old and who inevitably was a better player than you, knew the rules of golf better, and, of course, was much fitter than you. I soon found out why everyone had a caddie when I sliced a ball into the rough (I wasn't very good) and by rough, I mean mini-jungle. As I set off to find my ball, I was quickly stopped and told to give my caddie a nine iron and let him find the ball. Rather puzzled, I asked, "Why does he need a nine iron to find my missing ball?" and the reply came, "It's to scare off the snakes." They never seemed to find many of the lost balls, but one very cynical member swore he had bought back one of his own marked lost balls twice!

As I said in the chapter title, the social life in Lagos was great, but I got to the stage where I longed for a night in my flat with a good book. I don't mean to sound ungrateful for all the invitations I received, without which I would have gone mad. We Home Office reprobates were treated extremely well by our Foreign Office colleagues, and without their friendliness, there would have been a great number of us coming home before our secondment was over, and I thank everyone who I met for their kindness. Perhaps the biggest social event to take place during my time in Nigeria was the royal wedding of Prince Charles and Diana. We all received the following Invitation from the acting High Commissioner:

Mr R Howe

*On the occasion of the Wedding*
*of His Royal Highness the Prince of Wales*
*to Lady Diana Spencer*
*The Acting British High Commissioner*
*and Mrs T J Everard*
*Request the pleasure of your company*
*to cocktails at 18.30 hrs on 29 July 1981*

R.S.V.P.
611551 Ext. 151
Lounge Suit
National Dress

21 Ikoyi Crescent
Ikoyi

I can't remember too much of the evening. The champagne and drinks flowed, the canapés were more lavish than normal, and the national anthem seemed to be playing quite a lot. I was told the next day that I had introduced myself to the acting High Commissioner's wife in a "rather informal manner". No, I wasn't sent home in disgrace, I was just a little embarrassed, but nothing was said—Mrs E. was a very gracious lady.

My time in Lagos was one of the most interesting and harrowing periods I have ever spent. On one hand, some of the excursions we made were unforgettable, but I think that none of us would return voluntarily and being there without your wife and family could be very lonely.

*A break from Lagos.*

*Joseph—How I wish I had a steward at home.*

\*\*\*

# Chapter 14

## *The Social Side of Immigration*

About a third of Immigration Officers, at the time I was in the service, had been to university, but that didn't equate with sensible behaviour at all times. We had a great social life outside the office; a walking group and the five-a-side football fixture with the police is still held every Monday to this day after more than thirty years. During those years we had several well-known footballers kicking a ball about with us, Andy Goram, the Scottish goalkeeper, being a regular, and the number of newcomers and guest players, including my brother-in-law Robert Taylor, must have run into the hundreds. A few years ago, a celebratory get-together was arranged in Manchester for past and present players and there were over fifty guys who turned up with many more that were unable to attend. Another pillar of the social life at the airport was "the dominoes evening". This was, as most of our activities in those days were, an all-male affair, and was usually a great night out in a suitable hostelry. The whole thing came to an end when the ladies in the office tried to muscle in, putting their names on the list of those wishing to attend. A few of the harder drinking players thought it not suitable for ladies, and the evenings came to an abrupt end. Not very PC, I hear you say, but you must bear in mind that it wasn't until 1973/74 that women were allowed in the Immigration Service, and a great, much-needed civilising influence they were.

The other big activity was walking. We arranged a walk every month, ranging from the Cheshire Planes, the Peak District, Wales, and once a year a couple of days away in the Lake District. These away days were hilarious, as not all the participants came equipped in the right gear for what could be a hazardous undertaking, and no one in the group could read a compass properly, but despite all that we climbed most of the peaks in the Lakes and the only injuries sustained were usually alcohol-related.

Some of the places we stayed at in the Lakes left a lot to be desired from small B&Bs, and one time, when I lost the toss, I had to stay in a very old caravan in the garden of the B&B along with Ian Paterson, a fellow walker. The wind was so wild, we thought the caravan would surely be blown over. It was a long night.

On one visit to the Lakes, and thankfully it was one I missed, a group of the lads went for a Chinese meal. The service was so bad and the waiter so rude that some bright spark decided that the said waiter must be an illegal immigrant and on questioning him, it turned out the fellow was unable to prove he had permission to be here. He was promptly arrested and taken to the police station. Now this is perfectly fine and commendable when one is on duty and the restaurant has been targeted for a visit, but not when you are off-duty and have been indulging in the demon drink. This might have gone without much of a hitch if it hadn't been for another diner who just happened to be a friend of the owner and I think a solicitor to boot. The gentlemen made a complaint to the police, and guess what? He was also a friend of the chief constable of Cumbria. As expected, all hell broke out and a great many phone calls between the Immigration Service and the Cumbrian police were made, but after someone was sent to try and sort it out, and on establishing that the waiter did not indeed have permission to be in the UK, it was quietly forgotten.

There are so many tales involving my old colleagues that I would need another ten chapters to fit them all in. There was John Murrell, a Chief Immigration Officer who loved walking and cycling but whose main passion was gambling. (see chapter 12) When John retired he had several tragic events in his life and was unable to cope with them and ended his life. He is sorely missed by all his old friends and colleagues. I must also mention another CIO, one Brian Stone, who once almost got myself and Neil Rowland thrown off Stockport Golf Club halfway through a game. Brian was a nice man but a terrible golfer whose language, when he made a bad shot, was extremely colourful. At one point during this round, Brian sliced his ball into a sand bunker and was having great difficulty getting it out. Unfortunately, the ladies' captain and three ladies were playing a four ball behind us and we made the mistake of waving them through, forgetting that Brian was still in the bunker and attempting to call his ball every obscenity known to man. To this day, I have never heard so many tuts in my life.

One activity that briefly made an appearance in the office was jogging, but before you begin to think "That's healthy!", it was only to the Romper public house. In those days, when you could still see sheep from the office window and were able to jog around the runway perimeter, the pub was only some ten minutes of a slow jog away. We would exit the office via the luggage belt hall and on sunny days, the baggage handlers would sit outside during their break. One time, one of our female officers decided to join us, and on exiting the hall, suitably clad in shorts and a t-shirt, a huge cheer went up from the half-dozen handlers outside. However, the young lady wasn't very fit and had to return before reaching the Romper, and as she came back to the baggage hall we heard an even bigger cheer go up, much to her embarrassment. The young lady involved is now a very successful author and is featured in another part of the book when names will be named. This particular activity didn't last very long because it didn't take too long for us to realise that if you jogged there you had to jog back—not so enjoyable after a couple of pints.

Unlike a lot of people, I have always put a lot of emphasis on birthdays and have always tried to celebrate mine in a memorable place or by doing something a bit different. I can only recall having to work on my birthday on one occasion and that was when I was at sea. Both my thirty-fifth and fortieth were spent on canal boats, my thirty-fifth with four colleagues and their wives, and my fortieth with The Wheelers. The first trip was a very civilised affair with a barbeque and good behaviour all round, but the second was far more eventful. Both trips were on small self-drive boats holding up to ten people which you had to return before 6 p.m. For my fortieth, I supplied the booze, and each of my fellow bargees brought along food. Chris, Jackie, Trevor, Dave, Neil, Bea, plus Dave Fuller and myself, set off from Barbridge Marina near Nantwich and were lucky enough to have a glorious day for the trip. Trevor took charge of the tiller, the wine flowed, the food was magnificent, the sun shone, and all went well until a boatload of German tourists tried to pass us going the other way. By this time, we had got through quite a few bottles of Blue Nun, and there was a substitute captain at the wheel, who it has to be said had not passed his basic navigation course. With cries of "Don't mention the war!" and "Let's board them!" we narrowly missed their boat by inches and an international incident by seconds. A headline in the Daily Mail flashed by my eyes—
"BOATLOAD OF GOVERNMENT OFFICALS SINK

GERMAN TOURIST VESSEL". Apart from getting grounded a couple of times, the trip ended without further incidents and I had a very memorable birthday. On my fiftieth birthday I was in America visiting my brother Peter, who of course was to celebrate his forty-sixth birthday on the same day (see previous chapter). Peter at the time was Huntsman at the Mill Creek Foxhounds, just outside Chicago, and through a member of the hunt, who was a friend and also a stockbroker, he arranged for us to take a tour of the Chicago Stock Exchange. So, on our birthday in August 1992, we were on the actual floor of the exchange, and if I thought that hundreds of passengers made a lot of noise, I obviously hadn't been to a stock exchange before.

The canal boat theme also ran through the immigration social side, and I have been on a few trips with the "lads" which were very different from those where wives and girlfriends came along. For a start, a lot more beer was loaded up, and one of the activities during the cruise was cards. Now, cards can be an enjoyable way of passing time, but when combined with strong ale can lead to friction. This particular game of cards was going smoothly until the boat went through a rather long and dark tunnel. On emerging at the other end, one card player shouted that his stake money had disappeared and accused another player of taking it. It took a while to persuade the injured party that he had in fact lost his money on the last hand. Another such cruise nearly ended in disaster when one of the party fell overboard and disappeared under the boat, but happily resurfaced on the other side minutes after and was no worse for wear. On another trip, lunch was planned at a canal-side pub and, spotting our venue for grub, we moored up and walked to the garden of the designated public house. We settled in the few chairs and waited for someone to bring us menus and take our order, but all we could see was two people staring at us from the window of the pub! Only the pub was next door and we were sitting in a private garden. Happy days.

On occasions, the various airlines at Manchester held receptions or dinners to mark a new route or service. One such occasion was to celebrate Delta Airlines coming to Manchester and their new flight to Atlanta, the inaugural flight being on 7 June 1991. Normally, any invitation to these functions would be given to the inspector but on this occasion, he couldn't go and as I was the one who was handed the invitation, I was allowed to represent the department. A very good dinner was had by over 100 people, and as the invitation was for couples, my wife was with me. After the meal, the American CEO of Delta got up to make a speech and to draw a number for one lucky diner to win two tickets to anywhere that the airline flew to. The CEO congratulated the winning couple and turned to the other diners and asked if they thought the prize was a little mean. The response was predictable, so the CEO called for his station manager and shouted, "John—tickets for everyone." At this, uniformed airline staff appeared and handed everyone a letter which could be exchanged for two tickets to anywhere in the US via the Delta hub in Atlanta. This was great, but I was left with a dilemma—can I accept the free tickets, and do I have to declare them? The letter was in my name and could not be exchanged, so after talking to the inspector, who was very miffed he hadn't gone, it was decided that as the offer had been open to everyone there and couldn't be seen as some sort of bribe, I could use the tickets. A couple of months after, Linda and I were seated in first-class, having been lucky enough to have been upgraded on our way to Los Angeles via Atlanta.

Over the years, I went to lot of functions at the airport, but one that stands out was the time the Police Constable met the Chief Constable. At that time, the Airport Director was Gil Thompson who had worked for British Airways in Belfast in the past and knew one of my colleagues, John Graham, also from Belfast. John and I were on our way to the conference suite to attend (gate-crash) a drinks party, the reason for the function long forgotten, when we saw a young WPC who we had worked with on a couple of occasions. Although she was in uniform, we persuaded her to accompany us to the party. Unbelievable, but the first person we bumped into was the chief constable of Greater Manchester, James Anderton, also in uniform. The poor girl was mortified, the chief constable was mystified, and we couldn't stop laughing. Before questions were asked, Gil Thompson came over to say hello to John and the terrified WPC was able to make her escape, but she never spoke to us again!

\*\*\*

# Chapter 15

## *Retirement and Beyond*

Blessed retirement. The time came for my departure from Her Majesty's service and on 10 August 2002, I walked out of Manchester Airport a free and retired man. I'd like to say that my departure was to the sound of shouts of "Good luck", congratulatory handshakes from senior ranks, and maybe a small tear or two, but apart from the very sweet CIO on duty, Emma Jones, and the others on shift, I might as well have been leaving for the day. Oh, I did get a letter from the Home Office signed by an anonymous undersecretary to wish me well. It contained two mistakes, one on my length of service and one on the ports I had served at. I'm not bitter; well, yes, I am. A very small token of my thirty-eight years in government service would have been nice. However, I can console myself with the very acceptable final salary pension, the very happy time I spent at Manchester Airport, and the many good friends I made.

As was traditional in the Immigration Service, a retirement "do" was called for, and having the option of using the Delamere Park clubhouse, with all the facilities, I decided to hold it there. The thing that I was determined to dictate at the function was that there would be no speeches and no very senior officers attending. I would like to thank everyone who attended, and I was touched that the number of friends and colleagues, who had travelled some distance to be there, had had a good time. The food was certainly a hit as my good friend and interpreter, Jag Chadda, and I (with the help of my wife Linda) were responsible for the buffet. There were no speeches as such, but Dick Peg, a newly promoted Chief Immigration Officer, said a few very complimentary words, and all in all the evening was a success, as it was with some residents who were in the adjacent bar and were invited to help themselves to finish off the food.

In all honesty, I can't say that retirement came as a great shock as most of my former colleagues thought I had retired a couple of years earlier but just turned up each day for the craic. I often wondered what they thought that two-year demob chart on my desk was for! My wife Linda was still working at this time, so our future long-term travel plans had to be put on hold and I had to find something to fill my time. Having been a regular horse rider for many years, I thought that the Riding for the Disabled organisation may be able to use my meagre talents in that direction. So that was the start of a very happy time volunteering for that wonderful charity, and I was extremely saddened when a couple of years later I was forced out as a trustee of the local group over serious disagreements with the stable owners. Helping these poor kids was a pivotal time in my life and despite all the very serious disabilities I saw, the main emotion that came across was joy from the children, and laughter. However down I might have felt at the start of each session, I always went home with a smile on my face. The kids were amazing and really loved their time on a horse. I remember one time the little girl I was taking around the ménage, who on the first circuit whispered to me "I need the toilet", I couldn't see her mother, so I said, "I will find your mummy in a little while." She repeated her request on the next circuit, still no sign of Mum, so on the third time around she shouted, at the top of her voice, "I've weed my pants," bringing the whole ride to a stop amid much laughter at my embarrassment. The RDA is a wonderful organisation, as are the many volunteers working for them, and I have seen at first-hand how beneficial they are to the children and adults they help.

Horses have played an important part in my life and although I have never owned one, I have been lucky enough to know a lot of people who have but don't ride them much, and that's where I come in. From a friend who owned Major, a lovely big hunter, to the stables at Cholmondeley Castle, and for many years Snoopy and another Major owned by a colleague and stabled and looked after by Diane on her father's farm near Oulton Park. When I started riding at the stables of Cholmondeley Castle, I was usually accompanied by the son of the stable manager, Tony, but after a short time he trusted me to take a horse unaccompanied. The grounds of Cholmondeley Castle and Park are extensive and one of the nicest places to ride in Cheshire. To get to the parkland you have to pass close to the castle, the family home of the Marquess of Cholmondeley, and one of the sights I regularly came across was the Dowager Lady Cholmondeley exercising her dogs while driving with the leads out of the window and the dogs running alongside. I have much to thank Lady C. for, as she no longer rode but owned a really beautiful chestnut hunter of seventeen hands which needed exercising. When my colleague and fellow Wheeler, Jackie, bought Snoopy and had Major on loan, my riding increased, and I miss the times taking one of them around the gallops at Oulton Park. Sadly, all things come to an end and both horses, now quite old, passed away, but by this time my riding days had also passed. My one regret is that I never got to ride in Hyde Park, and as there is a weight restriction enforced by the nearest riding school of twelve stone, I guess I never will.

A couple of weeks before I was due to retire, the Commonwealth Games was being held in Manchester on 25 July to 4 August, and I thought that I would volunteer, the Home Office having agreed that staff could be released to take part. I duly attended the selection process and was taken on as a supervisor in the security section—bag and people searches. A short time later, I received my allotted post and was not impressed. I was scheduled to be at the City of Manchester Olympic Stadium at 6 a.m. each day and, as there was no parking, would have to catch one of the special buses from Manchester Central, all at my own expense. Now, I was used to early starts, but this would have meant leaving home at 4:30 a.m. each morning. I contacted the volunteer office and explained my predicament and suggested that perhaps my services could best be employed at the airport, where I would be the only volunteer with an airside pass and had access to all areas. In a flash, I was reassigned to the meet and greet team and given the job as a supervisor again. There followed some very pleasant two weeks where once again I was able to meet and chat to some very high-profile sports men and women. The big downside was the uniform we were required to wear; I took a lot of stick from my colleagues going around dressed in a very colourful tracksuit. Expecting masses of free tickets, I was very disappointed to receive only one—to the Greek wrestling competition! However, it was a nice change, and I got to keep the lovely tracksuit.

While I had been in full employment, I had dismissed several friends' attempts to get me to join the Masons, but with more time on my hands I thought I would give it a go. The two good friends who offered to sponsor me were Derek Thomas and Ray Connor, and so I entered the old chapel in Neston on the Wirral that housed The Cornerstone Lodge and thereby started nine years of very happy Freemasonry. My initiation into the craft was rather special as I was to be passed with three others, and this had never been performed in the Province of Cheshire before. The R.W. Provincial Grand Master of Cheshire, the top man, Timothy Raymond Roper Richards, came to attend the evening. All went according to plan, and in keeping when the top brass were present, the dinner after the ceremony, called the Festive Board, was extremely good. Cornerstone Lodge always put on a great Festive Board, none more so than at Christmas when Father Christmas put in an appearance, and the sight of the cream of the Wirral's business and professional classes greeting Father Christmas was a sight to behold. There was a very sad time at the lodge some years later when one of my fellow initiates and a lovely man, Alan Corney, was attacked outside his house when remonstrating with a young thug. He later died, I believe, as a result of his injuries, but the court thought differently and no serious charges were brought. Another very sad time to occur during those happy years was the suicide of Derek Thomas, who took his own life just days after the death of his wife from cancer. True gentlemen, as those two were, are rather short on the ground in today's world, and they are both sorely missed by the people who knew them. After nine years, the journey to Neston was getting to be a bit problematic, so Ray and I resigned from Cornerstone and joined a lodge in Frodsham. It is a much older lodge, with many elderly members, but it's just not the same and I don't get the same enjoyment out of a good dinner with like-minded gentleman. The venue for the Festive Board in Frodsham is the Old Hall, which was the first place Linda, my wife, and I went for a meal, and it never fails to bring back very happy memories. My good friend and fellow Mason Ray has carved a new career for himself after leaving the police and is now an actor; or rather, he has walk-on parts in TV shows. Some of those parts have been memorable. Who can forget Ray on a programme called *8 Out of 10 Cats*, where he comes on driving a mobility scooter wearing a pair of speedos and not much else? He is in his sixties; what a performer.

Since retirement, Linda and I have had a great many holidays and done a great deal of travelling. In 2016, we had twelve holidays or weekend breaks and completed twenty-four flights. In fact, sometimes I fear leaving the house as I can't guarantee that she hasn't booked another flight. The computer can be a terrible drain on one's resources, but more of that in a later chapter. Although I would not like to live in London again, I love visiting the place for a few days. I like to think that I know London quite well, and so when we go down for a visit, I like to explore a different part to the areas I know. One such bit was Islington, and I must confess, I was quite impressed with the choice of restaurants and the buzz of the place. When I was young, we were told that south of the river was a very dangerous place, full of muggers and pickpockets. Obviously, that's not true, and nowadays a visit to the South Bank gives you the wonderful Borough Market, the Tate Gallery, the Globe, and much more—a great area of London, and one which I love visiting. Another first was a trip on the Regent's Canal from Little Venice to Camden Market. The narrow boat ride passes the London Zoo, where you can stop off, and Camden Market is an experience not to be missed.

I don't want this chapter to turn into a travel guide to London, however, I must mention my mentor when it comes to London restaurants, the late and sadly missed A. A. Gill. Following his reviews in *The Sunday Times* gave us so many lovely meals in London, one of the best being

Zadels off Piccadilly: great French food, wonderful setting, and the prices won't frighten you.

Having travelled quite extensively from Manchester Airport for many years, I had got to know a lot of the staff and station managers, which proved very beneficial when checking in for a flight. In fact, I hardly ever had to turn right when getting on the plane, and Linda, my wife, thought it the norm for someone from the cabin staff to hand her a glass of champagne before she took her seat. Ryanair came as a great shock to her when I retired. While working at the airport we took quite a lot of flights to the USA, mostly to see my brother Peter who has lived there for a number of years. He has now taken American citizenship and lives in North Carolina with his Southern belle wife, a lovely lady called Suzanne.

Before Peter married his current lovely wife, he had been married a few times before, and I know he would agree with me that his second (or was it his third?) was a real horror. Despite this, we once had a great holiday with him when he was huntsman to The London Hunt Club in London, Ontario, Canada, where this young lady came from. I think one of the reasons Pete married her was that she looked good on a horse and could ride well. We had some good times riding in the beautiful countryside around London and have some very fond memories of these lovely horses.

Two of our very best friends are Andy and Jack Montgomery, who live on the island of Tenerife. They both had a passion to write for a living, and so ten years ago, they left their two highly paid jobs in the Civil Service (in fact, Andy was Linda's boss), spent six months attending the Spanish Centre in Manchester to learn Spanish, and went off to Spain to research the possibility of moving there. They settled on Tenerife, bought a lovely little *finca* on a banana plantation in Puerto de la Cruz, and started to write travel articles for any publication that would take them. They really struggled for a number of years but today they are highly respected travel writers with three books and a great many articles in half a dozen holiday brochures and newspapers to their names. We spend quite a lot of time each year in Tenerife, and its always one of the highlights of our visits to meet up with them for a very long lunch at one of the restaurants off the tourist areas that they have researched. For many years, both Andy and Jack were vegetarians, but on the road to Damascus (well, on their way to a sports bar actually) they had a metamorphic moment in the form of the smell of bacon frying. Since that moment, they have been avid foodies, and Jack's brilliant photographs both of food and scenery have graced many a publication. Jack is a very accomplished photographer and constantly finds his photographs ending up in articles that Andy has not written. I would urge anyone who wanted to see the "real Tenerife" to have a look at their website. It's so nice to see a lovely couple like Andy and Jack, who through hard work and persistence, achieve their dreams, a rare thing in today's world.

In the Eighties and Nineties, the Edinburgh Festival played an important part in our lives and we were lucky enough to have Linda's parents living close to the city centre as my father-in-law was stationed at HM Prison Edinburgh, or "Saughton", as it was known. For over ten years we visited my in-laws and took advantage of the free accommodation to visit the festival and enjoy the Fringe and other venues. Some of the big names of today started out at Edinburgh and we saw them when they were just starting out, comedians like Harry Enfield and Peter Cook, the Cambridge Footlights Revue, which produced John Cleese, and many more. I first saw Danny Boyle's *Trainspotting* as a stage play at the festival before it was turned into a film, and the original cast included Ewan McGregor and Robert Carlyle. The play was so raw and gripping that when the curtain came down there was some minutes before the stunned audience, including me, broke out in applause. I don't think I have ever forgiven my father-in-law when he was posted to Craiginches Prison in Aberdeen. In the last few years, the ridiculous hotel prices more than treble for the festival period and however much I miss it, I refuse to pay £200 pounds a night for a mediocre B&B in Leith. However, we do spend weekends in Edinburgh from time to time, and although I'm a great fan of London, my home town, Edinburgh is half the price with some really good restaurants. My only gripe is I can't use my bus pass.

You are what you drive. I know that's said to be what you eat, but it's a good introduction to write about some of the good, bad, and downright dreadful cars and motorbikes I have owned over the years, and I'll try to make it not as boring as some of the cars I've owned. One of the strangest cars I ever owned was a Rover 2000 which was bought from some friends of my father. Unfortunately, and very sadly, the husband committed suicide, and shortly after his wife did the same by attaching a pipe to the exhaust of the Rover and gassing herself in the garage. Quite naturally, their family wanted nothing to do with the car, and it was offered to me at a very reasonable price. The car was in wonderful condition and I'm not generally superstitious, so I bought it. After a few weeks of driving this really nice car, the windscreen wipers would start up, do a couple of swipes, and go off. This would happen four or five times a day, so of course I took it to a garage who tried a few things to cure the problem but without success. I then tried taking it to a Rover dealership who, after a couple of days testing and replacing various bits, announced that the problem was solved. No, it wasn't; the swiping returned within days. At this point, the car, which drank petrol at a great rate of knots, was costing me rather a lot and for that reason (honest, it was) I sold it in part exchange for something a bit less strange, but it really was a great car.

I suppose the most exotic car I ever owned was a Lotus Europa. Unfortunately, it was the model with a Renault 16 engine and spent as much time in the workshop as on the road. Luckily, I had the good fortune of having Spanns in Sandiway as my local garage, and even better, the place was owned and run by a certain Fred Spann. Fred was still working in his eighties and was the most fantastic mechanic you would ever meet. If someone brought in an old car for repair and the part was no longer available, Fred would get on his lathe and make it. One morning I picked up a colleague, Neil Rowland, to take to the airport, and as we drove along the dear old Europa kept surging alarmingly. We couldn't figure what was causing this until we noted that the accelerating rod or cable was under the passenger's feet and Neil had been moving his feet about, causing the car to accelerate. The next day, the car was back with Spanns, and a few days later, Fred phoned to say that it was fixed. He had completely run the cable in a different way and had had to make a few bits to enable this to be done. I can't imagine any of the big garages being able to do this today. Fred was a star motorbike racer in his younger days and a few years before he retired he was asked to compete in a veteran's race at Brands Hatch. Fred's nephew Simon later told me that Fred was not only able to get into his old leathers but went on to win the race, and he was the oldest competitor by quite a few years. On one occasion, Fred was looking at the cars in one of the big motor museums when one of the guides explained to him that the engine of his particular vehicle was rather special because it had some handmade parts which enhanced its speed. Although a modest man, Fred couldn't resist saying, "Yes, I know. I made them." A wonderful man, sadly no longer with us.

As have most drivers of my age, I have had a string of fairly unremarkable cars, and am certainly not a "petrol head". My real passion has always been for motorbikes. The last two bikes I owned were very different beasts indeed; a Suzuki Bandit and a Moto Guzzi.

The Suzuki was my pride and joy. I just loved that bike, but with age comes a slight slowing of reactions and I found it was becoming a bit too dangerous, and so I became seduced by an Italian, the Moto Guzzi Nevada. 750cc of sheer Italian attitude. The Nevada was at its best on a sunny day parked outside a trendy café being admired, but try to ride it in the rain and you were in trouble. It refused to start, and when you did get it going, it would sulk by missing a gear or two. In the end, I had to take it to the only dealership servicing Guzzis in North Wales, who promptly kept it for the next six weeks waiting for a part from Italy. When I got it back, I decided that this was the end of my time on a bike and put the machine on eBay. Of course, the bike looked great and I had no trouble selling it. A lawyer came over from Dublin, paid the asking price, and rode it back to Ireland. He later emailed to say how pleased he was with the bike. Although I'm now bike-less, I still visit Bill Smith's showroom in Chester for a drool over the latest models.

Music has played quite an important part in my life. I have rather cathartic tastes, from the early rock and roll to the classics. It may seem a bit macabre, but I have already selected the music I'd like played at my passing. The congregation (I expect there will be hundreds) will enter the cathedral (local church) to the *Marble Halls* song by Enya. The first hymn will be *The Day Thou Gavest, Lord, Is*

*Ended* by the King's College Choir, Cambridge (perhaps not in person). While the whole congregation (weeping copiously) reflect on my life and passing, Cecilla Bartoli (again, probably not in person) will sing *Casta Diva* from the opera *Norma*. The second hymn will be *For those in Peril on the Sea*, played by the Band of the Royal Marines (won't be able to fit them into the church, so they can broadcast from outside). Finally, as the people file out (thinking how privileged they have been to have known me) *Romance* (from *The Gadfly*) plays. I have thought long and hard about this, and I think that no more than twenty people should be allowed to give my eulogy. The wake can be held in St George's Hall, Liverpool, the cost to be born out of The Wheelers' bank funds (no refunds). Only Champagne Krug Clos d'Ambonnay 1995 is to be served and the food to be flown over from the Norwegian restaurant, Noma (Half of Robinsons bitter in the Tatton Arms with catering by KFC). If the fourth plinth in Trafalgar Square is still available—need I say more. In all seriousness, if the odd friend or colleague thinks kindly of me from time to time, that's all one can wish for. Still, St George's Hall sounds good.

*The other love in my life.*

*Jag and I tucking into some lovely Indian food.*

\*\*\*

# Chapter 16

## *The Wheelers*

In 1987, the cycling bug hit the office, and four of us went for the first ride that would be the start of an elite small group that is still going today, some thirty years later. John Murrell, Neil Rowland, myself, and Peter Cutch, a colleague from Heathrow who was visiting John, set out from Goostrey Station in Cheshire for a short ride around the countryside before a good lunch at a local hostelry. On that first outing, we covered some ten miles, but thought we had ridden in the Tour de France, and I can still taste that first pint; it was just wonderful. We always planned our rides around a good pub and over the years have sampled most of the best in Cheshire, and also our rides had to start at a nice café for coffee and more. The first ride we all think of as the start of The Wheelers was from Delamere Forest Station Café when Neil and I were joined by Chris Walling, Jackie Jarvis, Trevor Ogden, Dave Pemberton, Bea Latham, and Dave Nelson. During this ride, the name of the group was finalised as "Walling's Wheelers" in recognition of Chris's completion of that twenty-mile ride on a bike with only one gear working. Now just referred to as simply "The Wheelers", probably because he now has a couple more gears, the group has now branched out into spring and autumn breaks and spend a few days together both in the UK and abroad. Out of the eight original members, six of us are still cycling and going away together. Dave Nelson was posted abroad and never re-joined the group on his return, and Bea Latham sadly passed away in December 2014 and is greatly missed by all of us.

Over the years, we have done quite a few charity rides and we came up with the idea of raising some cash to donate, which was very successful. As we all worked at Manchester Airport, we thought that of the thousands of returning passengers, most of which will have some foreign currency that will just be put in a drawer and forgotten. We got permission from the airport authorities and an agreement from a bank in the airport to change the currency, so we set up collecting bins bedecked with a suitable notice asking for leftover foreign currency, and we were away. The response was incredible and we soon had bucket-loads of coins and notes to count. This is where our great colleagues in the office pitched in to help, and before long, some of the desks were covered in coins being sorted and stacked. In between flights, everyone gave a little time, and before long we were changing serious cash for charity. Now this idea has been adopted by most of the airlines and some airports, but I do believe that we were the first to come up with the idea, and I am proud to think that The Wheelers did their small bit for charity.

The whole idea of raising some money for charity came about with The Wheelers taking part in a ride for The British Heart Foundation. We also collected money on our other ideas, more of which later. The amount we raised put us in first place in a particular category and won us a trophy which was to be presented in London. On the chosen day, we all trooped down to London for a reception and the presentation and were quite surprised when William Roache (Ken Barlow, of *Coronation Street* fame) stepped up to make the presentation. I personally would have preferred Bet Lynch, but you can't have everything.

Other rides we did included several Manchester-to-Blackpool outings and a century (100 miles) ride. In fact, Chris and Trevor completed two of those and two coast-to-coast trips. I remember on one of those coasts-to-coast rides we stopped in the town of Hawes, and after a shower we all met up at about 7: 30 p.m. to go for a meal at one of the town's restaurants. I think there were eight of us, and we went into this nice-looking restaurant, which was less than half full, only to be told, "There are too many of you and the chef wouldn't be able to cope." We went to the other restaurant and had a great meal. I just wish I had taken a note of the name, but this was before Trip Advisor, so the first establishment got off without comment.

Our short breaks together have been very varied over the years. At first, we started going to the Lake District staying at a B&B just outside Hawkshead run by an ex-Fleet Street journalist called Eddy. Eddy was a real character and, what seems to be a running theme in this book, a man who really (no, really) liked his drink. A few years later, we switched to the Civil Service Country Club, Eaves Hall, near Clitheroe, where we happily went for many years until it was sold to a small hotel chain. In the first few years, we took our bikes, and then walking boots, and of course planned our walks around a good pub. Going back to Eaves Hall each year was like going home. It was old, rather grand, but a bit frayed around the edges. We got into a lot of silly competitions in the evenings—the best waistcoat, the silliest bow tie, and the loudest shirt. Sounds a bit childish, but when we all met up in the bar before dinner and had had a pre-dinner drink it was the funniest thing you could imagine. We would all mark each other from one to seven, and the winner was inevitably Bea, who made all her own bow ties, etc., and never disappointed in her outfits. Immigration Officers are generally not like most government service employees and at Eaves Hall it showed. I can only let you imagine some of the looks we attracted from the other more senior guests. On one visit to the hall, Dave, who had just returned from visiting one of his children who was working in Japan, came down for breakfast wearing a full Japanese pyjama suit— normal for Tokyo, but definitely not for the Civil Service County Club. We had some great times at the club and all miss being able to go there. The group still tries to meet up once a month for a short cycle ride but we are all retired now, with two of our members living in Yorkshire, so the winter weather and our growing age, me mostly, have rather curtailed those meetings to a good lunch.

Over the years, The Wheelers breaks have become more exotic, and for a few years now we have been taking both a spring and autumn short holiday. In the UK, our place of choice has been Ludlow in Shropshire, and we have been to quite a few cities in Europe courtesy of Jarvis Air. Jackie Jarvis, one of our small group, had married into a rather wealthy family, and the company they owned had at their disposal a private eight-seater Cessna jet.

Once a year, Jackie would arrange for us to use the plane to fly to a city of our mutual choice in Europe, hence the name "Jarvis Air". From 1999 to 2004, The Wheelers visited Brussels, Amsterdam, Berlin, Florence, and Verona, but sadly in 2005 the company sold the plane, incurring Trevor to blurt out, "What, they've got rid of our plane?". Our trip that year to Nice came as a great shock to us all, as we had to travel by Ryanair. But the high life was not all finished as, through Jackie's great generosity, we now go every summer for a few days to stay at her and husband's villa near Marbella. The most memorable trip we made in the Cessna was most definitely to Berlin. At the time of the visit, private aircraft could still land at Tempelhof Airport. The old terminal was originally constructed in 1927. Tempelhof was one of Europe's three iconic pre-World War II airports, the others being London's now-defunct Croydon Airport and the old Paris Le Bourget Airport. It acquired a further iconic status as the centre of the Berlin Airlift of 1948–49. One of the airport's most distinctive features is its massive, canopy-style roof extending over the tarmac, able to accommodate most contemporary airliners in the 1950s, 1960s, and early 1970s, protecting passengers from the elements. Tempelhof Airport's main building was once among the top twenty largest buildings on earth, and our first sight of the massive structure was jaw-dropping.

One of our "spring breaks", as we used to call them, was to Lisbon, and one evening we arranged to go to an old restaurant where there was folk dancing and fado singing. The meal was very ordinary and the folk dancing seem to go on and on, so much so that we decide to get the bill and adjourn to a local bar. However, the management insisted we stay for the fado singing almost to the point of locking the door, and how glad we were that they insisted. The singer who appeared was an elderly woman who we later learnt was a famous fado singer in Portugal and the younger sister of Amália Rodrigues, who was considered to be the best fado singer ever.

Amália Rebordão Rodrigues (23 July 1920–6 October 1999) was a Portuguese fadista (fado singer) and actress. Known as the "Rainha do Fado" ("Queen of Fado"), she was instrumental in popularising fado worldwide, and remains the best-selling Portuguese artist of all times.

Lisbon fado is the more well-known of the two styles of fado. This style has roots in social contexts that are set in marginality and transgression. It was frequently found in locations of sailors and prostitutes. In the early 1900s, it found a popular following that would continue to follow today.

We had a really nice visit to Lisbon until getting the bus to the airport to catch the flight home, when my pocket was picked and my wallet and passport stolen. Now, normally this would have entailed a visit to the British Embassy and a two- or three-day wait for checks to be made back in the UK, but luck was really with me in the shape of a dear old colleague, Denise Beddows, who just happened to be stationed at the Lisbon Embassy, and even better was the Airport Liaison Officer. Denise was marvellous, making a lot of phone calls both to the airline and to the immigration authorities in Lisbon and Manchester to arrange a hassle-free return home. Denise took early retirement after serving in HM Immigration Service and in various posts abroad with the Diplomatic Service. She is now a very successful author, writing under her maiden name, D. J. Kelly. Denise has published two novels, *Running with Crows - The Life and Death of a Black and Tan*, and *A Wistful Eye - The Tragedy of a Titanic Shipwright*, who was in fact her great grandfather; both extremely good reads. She has also written several historical books based around Chalfont St Peter, where she lives with her husband Terry, who is also a friend and an old colleague. By now, Denise will, I'm sure, have published many other books, but I can never thank her enough for coming to my aid all those years ago.

Another first for The Wheelers was a tour of the House of Lords in July 2006. This was laid on by George, a relative of Chris Walling, and conducted by Brian, Lord Mackenzie of Framwellgate, who had risen through the ranks of the police force to become a Chief Superintendent and President of the Police Superintendents Association. He confided to us that it had come as a bit of a shock when Tony Blair had asked him if he would like a seat in the Lords on the Labour benches. We all had a great day with drinks on the terrace after the tour, and Brian turned out to be a pleasant host. It's quite uncanny to walk round that iconic building and see many of the famous faces you see on TV. The day ended with Brian presenting everyone with a copy of his book, *Two Lives of Brian*. Since that tour, Brian has not been without some controversy and was temporarily suspended from his seat in the house, but I don't want to dwell on that. He certainly gave The Wheelers a great day out.

One of our cycling heroes, who happens to be a colleague, was the IO Eric Jackson, previously mentioned and known as Mr Salford due to him being the last full-time Immigration presence at Salford Docks. Eric cycled to the airport and back every day, a distance of some fifteen miles each way, and also went cycling on his days off and holidays. When he retired, he cycled across America from coast to coast, and some of the tales he told of that journey made The Wheelers' rides look like a stroll around the park. He got together a serious of photo slides of his trip and began giving talks to the WI and other groups. He claimed that he had not bought himself a drink in over a year as there were always plenty of ladies to stand him a pint or two after the talk. In the days Eric worked at Salford Docks, he had a very small office just inside the dock gates. It consisted of a tiny room with a small desk, a chair, a gas fire, and a kettle. There was an even smaller reception room with a hatch for the ships' agents, etc., to hand in their manifests and chat to Eric. He was very well-known by all who used the docks, and I suspect that, come Christmas, Eric would not have to buy himself whisky for some time after. I often wonder what he would have made of the area that now is Media City.

In the late Seventies, I took up skydiving. I think I must have seen the passing of time and thought, "If I don't do it now, I never will." I contacted the Manchester Parachute Club and arranged to undertake the two-day training course. Understandably nervous, but the standard of training was so good and the instructor was the most charismatic guy you could wish to meet, I think that I would have jumped without a parachute if he had said that it was safe to do so. Like so many of the skydiving instructors, he was ex-military and was perfect at his job. On 15 May 1977, I made my way to Forton Drop Zone in Shropshire to make my first descent. The plane was a Cessna 172 with the door off and a small metal platform over the wheel. This aircraft took the pilot, of course, the instructor, and three jumpers, including one very nervous first timer, me. The worst part of this activity, in my opinion, is stepping out onto that small platform at 2500 feet. The wind speed, which was recorded in my log as 8 MPS, hits you like an express train, but when the instructor shouts "GO!" your training kicks in; you fall backwards and start counting until the parachute opens four seconds later. The adrenaline rush is like nothing I had ever experienced and when you land safely it's an amazing feeling, which, unfortunately for your wife and friends, you talk about non-stop for the next twenty-four hours. While I was floating down, the wind suddenly changed and took me some distance from the drop zone. I landed unceremoniously in a ploughed field and was dragged fifty feet or so before I could gather up my parachute. By the time I had walked to the road, the club's van had arrived to pick me up, but I was on such a high I would not have cared if I had had to walk back to the drop zone. I made three other jumps after that, two at Forton and later one with the Cheshire Parachute Club at Tilstock. Skydiving for novices like myself can be very frustrating as you are dependent on the wind being below a certain speed and clear visibility before you are allowed to jump, so for many Sundays we drove to the drop zone, waited about all day, and returned home without getting to parachute. I got to love the few times that the weather was favourable, but it was unfair and boring for my wife. It's advisable to have someone to drive you home "just in case", so I decided to end my skydiving career. However, some years later I floated the idea to get a team from the Immigration Office to make a parachute jump to raise money for charity, and five others agreed to take part. Those who took part were Dave Pemberton, Dave McDonough, and Fiona Jack from the Immigration Office, Maggie, a girl from airport security, a friend, Ben McDyre, and myself. We all managed to get a jump in, but unfortunately Dave P. broke a toe on landing and Fiona, being seven stone ringing wet, took so long to descend that she narrowly missed landing on the runway as the plane was coming into land. We all enjoyed the day but, to my knowledge, no one has repeated the experience.

With all of us now in our senior years, the cycling has been somewhat curtailed, but we do still try to meet up for lunch on the first Thursday in the month. With two of our group now living in Yorkshire, this usually means just the four of us. However, the "Yorkies" try to join us as and when they can, and we still have our annual trips together.

*The way we were*
*Left to right: Bea, Dave N, Trevor, Jackie, Neil, Chris, and me.*

*Chris, William Roache, Jackie, and myself.*

*L to R: Dave McDonough, Fiona Jack, and me.*

\*\*\*

# Chapter 17

## *France—Where I Daily Eat My Own Body Weight in Cheese*

For the past seven years, we have been very lucky to have some great friends, Alan and Val Burnham (cousins to Andy Burnham, the new Mayor of Manchester), who own a lovely old farm house in the Dordogne, and we have been able to spend some of our summers there keeping an eye on the house. During that time, we have met some wonderful people who live in the area. Tony and Ann, an ex-Squadron leader and theatre sister; Paul, a retired Metropolitan Police Officer, and his lovely wife Ann, an ex-school teacher who speaks perfect French; John and Carole, Australian teachers who spend many months in France; Richard and Anne Hand; and a lot of other casual friends. The house is some twenty kilometres from Bergerac and is in a quiet little hamlet called Beleymas. On leaving Bergerac Airport and stopping off at the supermarket on the way, we can be sitting beside the pool sipping some of the regions wonderful rosé wine within the hour. Val and Alan very kindly let us have a few relatives and friends stay for short periods, and this just adds to our enjoyment at staying at Laurie, the house name.

One of the great things about this region are the markets, and we spend a lot of time shopping for fresh food, sitting outside cafés, and generally watching the world go by. One of the best markets is held in Issigeac on Sunday morning. This is a beautiful little town and, on market day, becomes alive with noise and colour with stalls selling everything from live chickens to oysters and all the clothes you could wish for. Sitting at one of the outside cafés with a café creme is people-watching heaven and one of the things that make France so special.

However, our greatest joy is having dinner or just drinks with our friends. I never realised before that dinner could take five or six hours and be over in a flash. Laurie is very old with stone walls some two-feet thick, and, being so old, has its share of birds, mice, and lizards living in the roof space, but we were not prepared to be joined one visit by a four-foot black snake.

The Aesculapian snake (*Zamenis longissimus*) is a species of non-venomous snake native to Europe, a member of the family Colubridae, and growing up to 2 metres (6.6 feet) in total length (including tail), it counts among the largest European snakes.

After the initial shock and furious research on the internet, we were mightily relieved to discover that our snake was not harmful and very docile. On the very odd occasion that we could hear it slithering about in the loft, we found that the mice population, which was far more annoying than the snake, had all decamped and moved out.

The nearest town of any size from the house is Mussidan, which is some twelve kilometres away and was brutally dealt with by the occupying Germans in the Second World War. The account I have been told is that three German soldiers were taking two French women, who had been injured, to their field hospital for treatment when the vehicle they were travelling in was ambushed by the French Resistance. The Resistance killed the soldiers and shot the women, who they took to be collaborators. As a reprisal, the Germans rounded up fifty of the town's men and shot them. I can't vouch for how near the truth this account is. The actual official version is this: On 11 June 1944, a detachment of the Sipo-SD, commonly known as the "Gestapo", reinforced by a platoon of the North African brigade, shot fifty-two people in Mussidan, including Raoul Grassin, the mayor of the town, in retaliation for an attack by the resistance on an armoured train in Mussidan station, and an attack on a convoy of the eleventh Panzer Division of the Wehrmacht.

Mussidan seems to have a rather sad atmosphere as, along with many towns in France, it is suffering an economic downturn. However, it has two great advantages for us: a beautiful old church that has been converted into a lovely little cinema, and the Auberge Du Musee, a restaurant run by Valerie and Bertrand St-Martin, a sweet couple we now call friends. The Cinema Notre Dame shows English language films twice a month, and it is a real pleasure to sit in this beautifully converted old building, complete with the original beams, and forget for a few hours the fact that you have just ignored your cardiologist's advice by consuming a wonderful French meal of some 5000 calories. We came across the Auberge Du Musee on our first trip to France when we were sampling the various restaurants in the area. There were four of us, and after a very nice dinner we paid the bill and departed, but on looking at the receipt at home we saw that the restaurant hadn't charged us for any drinks and, as we had run up a fair amount on wine, it was decided to phone the restaurant and inform them that we would call in the next day and settle up. Valerie, who we spoke to, said that she would be visiting her mother the next day and would be passing our house so would call in. She duly arrived along with her three absolutely beautiful daughters aged between four and seven and a bottle of the local rosé. On departure, all three little girls had to kiss all of us on both cheeks. The custom is so nice that I think that this was the point when I knew that France would be on my itinerary for as long as I was able to travel. We have been going to the Auberge Du Musee now for six years and have seen the girls grow, but if they are at home on our visits, they still appear to greet us and make us feel as if we are part of the St-Martin family.

In this area of France there are not as many restaurants as one would imagine, or, indeed, would like, but one that deserves a mention is La Truffe D'Or in St Mayme de Pereyrol. This lovely little restaurant is run by two English gentlemen, Jonathon, who serves, and Simon, the chef. Simon was classically trained in some of the top restaurants in Paris and quite frankly produces some of the best food in this part of the Dordogne. Jonathon's friendly service and the wonderful food are reasons enough for us to visit several times during our stay in France each year. Another one of our favourite restaurants is called Le Chat Perche, and every Friday night they have an evening of *à volonté*. It is always huge amounts of prawns or mussels served with piles of chips, and when you have eaten the first amount you call out to the waitress "*À volonté!*" and she brings you a further large helping. In the six years of going to this restaurant, I have never seen anyone ask for a third helping, and that includes the many French lorry drivers that frequent the place on Fridays.

One thing you don't see every day in the UK is the "pig in the garden" incident. This happened while the Burnhams, the house owners, were in residence. Hearing a terrible noise early one morning, Alan looked out of the window to see a huge black pig rooting about in the flower bed. He called the mairie (town hall) and spoke to the local mayor, who said that he would send help. This arrived a short while after and, after a lot of discussion and much hand waving, they were unable to identify the owner of the pig, so they shot it. While they were standing around discussing who they would get to butcher the animal and which cuts each man would like, a car pulled into the drive and a man got out, shouting, "You've killed my pig." All thoughts of Alan getting a nice leg of pork disappeared (traditional, if game is killed on your property in rural France) when the men loaded the carcass into the poor fellow's car and he drove off. Hunting is very big in this part of the Dordogne. The woods in the area hold deer, wild boar, and lots of other edible creatures. During the season from September, one sees lots of small groups of men with rifles slung over their shoulders standing at the edge of woods wearing fluorescent jackets. Every year, several hunters are shot by mistake, so I think the loud outerwear is something of a necessity.

One year, we arrived earlier than usual in May. Now, this is the Dordogne in France—it's warm and sunny, surely? Wrong. This particular May was cold and wet and we had arrived with shorts and t-shirts. Not wanting to spend a lot of money on clothes we didn't really want, our friends told us of an institution in France called the *friperie*. These are held in village halls and consist of piles of second-hand clothes. One pays six euros on the door and is given a black plastic bag which you can fill to bursting. Linda duly set off and returned some time later with two sweatshirts, one jumper, one pair of tracksuit bottoms, a coat, and various bits and pieces. Cold problem sorted, and I still have one of the sweatshirts in a box in France.

Over the years we have been pleased to ask some of our friends and relations to join us for a few days. Sylvia and Robert Taylor, Linda's sister and her husband, Heather and Neil Rowland, my old colleague, Linda's girlfriend, Chris Garner, and, sadly, our departed and oldest friends Val and Alan Pugh. Two other friends who regularly join us for a few days are Ros and Keith Trenell who we see a lot of back in the UK. Keith is incredibly kind in giving us lifts to the airport when we depart for our many holidays each year. It is supposed to be a reciprocal arrangement, but poor old Keith seems to have drawn the short straw as he picks us up far more than we take him, but it's so nice to be met after a long flight by Keith's friendly face and I'm immensely grateful to him and Ros. At a certain time of the year, the house is surrounded by fields of sunflowers and our guests are always amazed by this beautiful sight. It's one that puts a smile on even the most serious of faces and is always appreciated by our guests.

In 2016, the Tour de France was scheduled to pass right by Laurie, but unfortunately, I was due to return to the UK the day before it happened. Alan and Val had returned to France and were greatly looking forward to hosting a small party for friends at the edge of their land which was only separated from the tour route by a small strip of grass. Just before the riders were due, Alan and his party moved their picnic tables to the viewing spot, only to discover that the local mayor had given permission for several food stalls to set up on the grass verge. With a lot of other onlookers setting up BBQs and picnic tables on the verge, poor old Alan was forced to leave the great position in his garden and join the rest of the public on the verge. I believe that a good time was still had by all and I didn't feel quite so bad for missing a great party. Having been a keen cyclist, I have always taken an interest in the Tour de France and indeed the Tour of Britain, and whenever possible have travelled to a city or town where I could watch the tour pass by. The cavalcade of sponsors' lorries and vans, plus all the support vehicles, really heightens the atmosphere, and if you're lucky you may grab a hat or even a t-shirt. It really is one of the great sporting events. In talking to our "French" friends over the years, we came to know the things they missed in

France and, as you would expect, there was a very diverse list, but the few things that came up time and again were British sausages and bacon. So, for the past few years we have lugged a case stuffed full of sausages, smoked bacon, and black pudding. On the first Sunday of our return to France, we invite all our lovely friends to a full Anglo-British/French brunch, the French bit being the eggs, mushrooms, croissants, and of course a few glasses of their version of prosecco, champ-something or other. We have got quite used to the three-hour lunch and the six-hour dinner, but the four-hour brunch was completely new to us and all the more enjoyable for it.

I have always been fond of my food and have for many years told people that the only two things I would have to refuse to eat are whelks and tripe. I think my food likes are quite extensive and I'm ever ready to try new dishes and recipes, which sometimes backfires on me. The time I was trying to impress my wife and took her to La Basola in Liverpool and ordered the steak tartar (raw minced beef with a raw egg in the middle). I do most of the cooking at home and have to say, apart from the day-to-day meals, I thoroughly enjoy doing so. The whole process of planning a menu, shopping for the food and cooking for friends can be very rewarding. At the moment, my standard menu is based on dishes that are tried and tested:

- Salmon and crab in a garlic cheese mould
- Pork medallions in a tarragon cream sauce
- Cherry pancakes or filo pastry tarts in amaretto cream
- Cheese and oatcakes

I keep lists of menus served to everyone having dinner at chez nous. This avoids repeating dishes but makes it difficult to come up with new menus taking into account friend's dislikes. One of the easiest dishes to serve are small pancakes or crêpes, served as a starter filled with garlic mushrooms, buttery or creamed seafood, or a mild goats' cheese, and as a pudding filled with cherries, chocolate sauce, or just with a squeeze of lemon and brown sugar. I try to create menus and food from a particular country, French, Italian or Spanish, and I have found that a table of tapas dishes, where everyone just digs in, is very popular and not difficult to put together. My personal favourite is scrambled eggs cooked with black pudding—Stornoway, not Bury, I'm afraid (sorry Lancastrian friends). We have had the "Where is the best black pudding made?" argument for many years, and I have been firmly on the side of Bury, but finally had to admit that the texture and subtle taste of the Scottish pudding is the best.

Food and restaurants in the UK nowadays easily rival their French counterparts and the rise of "gourmet" pubs is a tremendous step forward. However, a good old traditional establishment with well cooked "pub grub" takes a lot of beating. Another real plus, in my opinion, is the increase in food markets with pop-up stalls and street food with some very imaginative dishes. We in the north-west are lucky enough to have quite a few foodie places to eat, but the ones I have sampled are Altrincham Market, Knutsford Market, and the Baltic Market in the old Cains Brewery buildings in Liverpool. The market in Altrincham is housed in the old Victorian market hall and has rejuvenated the heart of this original market town, whose charter dates back to 1290. Around the outside of the hall are more than half a dozen food vendors with trestle tables in the centre. Knutsford, also in Cheshire, holds a wonderful market on the first Sunday of each month. The food part of the market, where you can sit down to eat, is small compared with the other two, but the food available on the stalls is unbelievable. Over ten pie and pastry stalls, dozens of cake stalls, local gin and beer outlets, the best sausage stall anywhere, and many more, and all this with a very accomplished jazz band to serenade you. One can put on half a kilo of weight just walking down one side of the market. Opened this year (2017), the Baltic Market is a revelation, housed in the giant Cains Brewery complex. It is a true foodie paradise and is full of amazing street food brands. Cains Brewery was founded in 1858 by Robert Cain but in 1921 he sadly died and some decades later the brewery closed. It was left derelict for many years but is now full of bars, coffee shops, and vintage outlets. Some of the food on offer is amazing, from spicy lamb samosas to soft shell crab burgers with halloumi fries (a regular sitting next to me said that people came from far and wide to sample these halloumi fries), popcorn mussels, and, for our veggie friends, a rainbow Rasta bowl of various vegetables with coconut quinoa. All I'd really like now is someone to come up with a pill to counteract all the calories eaten.

On the subject of France and food, I can't help noticing over the years that the rise of the dreaded burger, pizza, and fast food chains has increased alarmingly. It's also sad to see that a lot of France's young seem to have abandoned their gourmet heritage and now seem to prefer fast food. On our latest visit to France in July of 2017, we learned that for various reasons, Alan has put the lovely house on the market. Realising that this was more than likely to be our last stay at Laurie was very sad, and even more so when all our "French" friends told us of how much they looked forward to our visits and how much they will miss us. However, we are determined to return next year on some basis and have already looked at a few gîte possibilities for the future. Those last few weeks just flew by and were filled with wonderful dinners at our friends' houses, a picnic by the beautiful river Dordogne, the spectacular firework display on Bastille Day, and a *marche gourmande*, which is a gathering of locals and visitors held in a field with trestle tables and stalls selling great BBQ food. I have been to many of those functions over the last seven years and have always been impressed by the behaviour of the young people. There is a lot of wine consumed during the evening, but not once have I witnessed any thuggish behaviour, and everyone has a good time. During those few weeks, there were several viewings of the house, and we tried to tell the prospected buyers that the house was damp, the roof needed replacing, it has snakes in the loft, we had been burgled five times in two years, it's very noisy, and other encouragements (only joking, Alan), but all on deaf ears. The house is lovely and everyone said so. This, then, is probably the end of an era, and I must thank all those wonderful friends for their really great friendship and hospitality over the years, the Wrights, the Edwards, the Hands, and, of course, the Burnhams, for helping to give us the opportunity to experience France at its best.

*Laurie*

*Good food, good wine, and good friends.*

\*\*\*

# Chapter 18

## *More Holidays and Travel*

When I look back on some of the many holidays we have had over the years, I think, "Did I really do that?". Having been in the Merchant Navy, I had been to a lot of the destinations that I returned to in later life and learnt one thing: never expect previous places visited to remain the same. Linda got thoroughly sick of me saying, "I'm sure that seventeenth century church wasn't there before." Istanbul was a case in point, as one of the places I took Linda back to of course hadn't changed in hundreds of years, but I swear that the Blue Mosque was in Taksim Square in 1962. We were staying in Bodrum, in the Mugla province, of the southwestern Aegean region of Turkey, on a two-week holiday in a little hotel next to the biggest and certainly loudest open-air disco in Europe, the awful Halikarnas. After five nights without sleep, I came up with the bright idea to visit Istanbul and find a quiet place to stay and get a good night's sleep. Enquiries at the hotel came up with the information that you could get a bus from the town centre to Istanbul. Great, couldn't take that long! Fifteen hours, that's how long, but with the wonderful city of Istanbul to look forward to, it went quite quickly.

We found a reasonable hotel in Taksim Square (still can't believe that the Blue Mosque wasn't on the corner) and set about seeing the sights. Of all the fantastic sights to see in Istanbul, for me the most interesting one is the Basilica Cistern. The Cistern is the largest of several hundred ancient cisterns that lie beneath the city. Located 500 feet southwest of the Hagia Sophia, it was built in the sixth century during the reign of Byzantine Emperor Justinian. The cistern was used as a location for the 1963 James Bond film *From Russia with Love*, and was featured in the climax of the Dan Brown novel *Inferno*.

On the afternoon before we were scheduled to catch the horrendous bus back to Bodrum, we were strolling through the Grand Bazaar when a young man approached us and asked, in perfect English, if he could have a word with us. He explained that he was a student at Manchester University and was currently on holiday helping his father run the family carpet business. He added that he had been sent out to try and persuade tourists to visit his father's shop and would we consider just looking at the carpets, of course, no obligation to buy, and this would show he had been doing what his father had asked of him. I like to think that I am somewhat streetwise and knew a scam when I saw one, but for reasons I can't explain, we agreed and were lead up a side street to a very small carpet shop. We met the father, who called for apple tea and proceeded to show us some really wonderful Turkish carpets. Of course, the inevitable happened, and Linda fell in love with a beautiful traditional rug. I put up all the arguments I could think of— it cost too much, it's too big to get on the flight home, I don't have enough money on me to pay for it, all to no avail. The price came down, it was folded small enough for hand luggage, and the student son knew of a cash machine in a bank just around the corner. It really was a lovely carpet, so I abandoned my poor wife to drink more tea with the old man, never thought that she may have been wrapped in a carpet and exported to someone's harem in my absence, and got the cash to pay for the goods. The carpet is still in everyday use and still looks great.

We have been to the USA on numerous occasions, but the most eventful visit was a road trip to Los Angeles and around California to Las Vegas. While in San Diego, we decided to cross the border and spend a couple of days in Tijuana, Mexico. Having a hired car, we were told, "Do not under any circumstances take the car into Mexico as you will not be insured or even legal." We were also advised to park in one of the huge carparks just before the border controls. After driving around for ten minutes, I noticed that the uniforms of the police looked a little different to what we had come to expect. And yes, you guessed it, we had slipped into Mexico. A quick turnaround had us back at the border post and facing a very mean looking border guard. The conversation went thus:

Border Guard: How long have you been in Mexico?

Me: About five minutes.

BG: Don't be smart with me, fellow.

Me: No, you don't understand—we made a mistake.

BG: You certainly did. Get out of the car!

Me: I'm sorry. Can I explain?

BG: You've got a lot of that to do, so start talking.

After I explained what had happened and, more importantly, that I was in fact a fellow officer from across the pond, the border guard, now known as Ted, was charm itself. He was being posted to Dublin in a few weeks (the US have an immigration office at Dublin Airport to process passengers flying to the USA) and as he had never left the States before, he was full of questions. We chatted for about fifteen minutes and the queue behind my car stretched as far as you could see, but Ted seemed far more interested in my knowledge of Ireland. We parted firm friends and I said a silent prayer of thanks to the gods of fate for directing me to HM Immigration Service years ago.

Unfortunately, that wasn't the only brush with the US law enforcement fraternity I had during that trip. One afternoon we were in Orlando looking for a particular shopping mall, with my wife navigating and me driving, when she suddenly shouted, "It's there on the right!" Of course, my reaction was to immediately obey her by making a right turn, unfortunately not into the mall but into the side of another car. Luckily no one was hurt, but the two ladies in the other car said that under the law they were obliged to call the police. Some ten minutes later a highway patrol car pulled up and one of the biggest (around the waist, not in height) police officers I had ever seen strolled over and, after taking a few details from the lady driver, asked me to accompany him and sit in his car while he wrote me a ticket. Seeing this, my wife started to think that I was being taken to some hellhole of a jail and got more worried as the time went on. In the meantime, I was shifting a small arsenal of guns from the front seat so as I could sit in the passenger seat of the police car. The policeman turned out to be very friendly and I can't recall what brought it up, but the conversation turned to famous arrests he had made. By this time, I had confessed my occupation and countered his famous TV star arrest with my encounter with James Brown, the singer. Well, he stopped writing the ticket and shook my hand and said why had I not told him this before he started to write the ticket as he would have waved the offence, but the tickets were numbered and he now had to issue it. Obviously not a James Brown fan. It cost me sixty dollars which I sent by post three weeks later, and as I'm sure you will agree, this incident was entirely my wife's fault.

In the Seventies and Eighties, skiing played a big part in our holiday choice, and for six years we tried to go on a skiing trip each year. Austria, France, and Italy were all given a try, but for me, Austria will always come out on top. Seefeld was the first resort we went to and I think that it was probably the best holiday we had. I think you have more fun in a beginner's class than subsequent classes, which are taken more seriously, and in Seefeld we had a great deal of fun. In the beginner's class there is no expectation of you and everyone falls on a regular basis. In our group of ten there were three nationalities and ages ranging from twenty-three to sixty, and we even liked each other to the extent that we all met up in the evening. On the last skiing holiday, we went on, I started to have trouble with one of my knees and found it hard and painful to make a left turn. Not a good situation to be in while on a black run. After struggling for a few days, I made the decision to give up skiing for the rest of the holiday and started to appreciate the joys of sitting in the sun at a mountain café with a glass of hot *gluhwein* and an Ian Rankin book. Bliss.

Another rather eventful holiday was to Crete in the late Seventies. In those days, I did all the flight and hotel bookings myself and usually tried to charm the holiday reps into letting us ride to our nearest destination in the transfer coach. An airport pass got us onto the coach and we were dropped off in Heraklion town centre. We quickly found our hotel only to find that they didn't, so they said, have a booking, and the hotel was full. They did, however, offer us beds on the flat roof of the hotel, and as it was nearing midnight and a warm night, we accepted. We shared the roof with one other couple and had a reasonable night's sleep, but in the morning found ourselves the main entertainment of the day. Our rooftop bedroom was surrounded by taller buildings and we were a source of great hilarity to our neighbours. To add insult to injury, when we took the lift to the ground floor with the couple who had shared our rooftop bedroom, the lift gave a few shudders and then plummeted to the ground. Luckily for us, a breaking mechanism stopped the lift from smashing into the basement and after ringing the alarm and shouting for some ten minutes, the manager came and forced the door open and we crawled out between the floors. Rather than apologising and offering us free accommodation, meals, or cash for our frightening experience with his worthless old lift, he started to rave and shout at us in Greek. It was not until he pointed out the notice outside the lift stating that the maximum capacity of the lift was three people that we understood his anger. Needless to say, we only stayed the one night of the two "booked", and the hotel only charged us half the room rate! We caught the bus to Hersonissos and had some very pleasant two weeks' stay in a very basic B&B called Nicks, but the restaurants overlooking the beach made up for any lack of amenities at the B&B.

One of the very first holidays that Linda and I went on together was to Bulgaria in the early Seventies, to a wonderful place called Sunny Beach! What on earth possessed us to choose Bulgaria is still a mystery to me, but I do remember that the beaches looked good, it was cheap, and it had the added attraction that all the hotels gave out vouchers so you could eat in any one of their restaurants. Nice touch, but they failed to tell you that the food and menus in every one of the hotels was identical and the food was awful. Poor Linda lived on the Bulgarian equivalent of a Greek salad for fourteen days. The resort, and I use that term lightly, was full of very large Russians, and as you were not allowed to venture out of the place in those days, car hire being non-existent and local transport unthinkable, you were stuck with the beach during the day and dinner at night. One evening we decided to splash out three vouchers instead of the usual two and go to what we were told was the best hotel in the resort—this merely meant that you got a paper napkin and a fork with your dessert spoon. All looked okay and we both started with the almost obligatory, I think it was called, Shopska salad, and waited for our main course. After some ten minutes, all the waiting staff and one or two chefs came and sat at one of the tables in the restaurant, started loosening their jackets, and handed out cigarettes. After another fifteen minutes, they got up and service was resumed—the peoples' working fag break seen at its best. The other memorable memory of this holiday occurred one morning at about 7:30 a.m. when we were woken up by smoke bellowing under the bedroom door; there was a gap of some six inches. Rushing out of the room in any clothing we could grab, thinking that the place was ablaze, only to find that the hotel staff were merely carrying out the weekly fumigating routine.

In the late Sixties, I had a holiday in the former Yugoslavia, staying at a large hotel just along from Dubrovnik. This was at a time when Marshal Tito was the President, and before the country was torn apart by the civil war that saw it split into various republics. We must have been on a very cheap package deal as the room we were allocated was in the basement with only a tiny window high in the wall. I had not suffered an asthma attack for some ten years but one night in that room saw me wheezing like an old steam engine and a doctor was called. A nice doctor in his early thirties arrived and promptly ordered the hotel manager to change my room to one on the top floor, and lo and behold, that was the end of my asthma attack but not the friendship with the doctor. When he called the next day to check on my condition he was accompanied by his wife, and being so grateful for the room upgrade, I invited them to lunch. They were such a nice couple and we enjoyed their company tremendously. They must have thought the same as they invited us to dinner at their apartment the next evening. Dr Marko Petrovic and his wife, Mina, lived in a small apartment on the first floor of a large block. We were made very welcome and, with a great deal of pride, Marko explained that the drink we were about to have was made by his father in the country to an old family recipe and called Slivovitz. It was made from damson plums and often referred to as plum brandy. My first taste of Slivovitz was not a great experience; I thought it was the foulest thing that I had ever tasted, but given the circumstances I had to finish the horrible brew. My salvation came (I thought) in the way of a small balcony overlooking the street where I gently tipped the drink over the edge. Marko was so pleased that I liked his family brandy so much I had finished it so quickly that a refill was soon in my glass and I was forced to get it down. Marko was an anaesthetist at the local hospital who on his time off was retained by several of the local hotels to be on-call. It was rather ironic that at the time of this holiday I had just ended my six months "medical career" as a student theatre technician and had been earning more than the doctor was at the time. Mark explained that the one thing he couldn't get in Yugoslavia was suitable shoes to wear in the operating theatre, which he described as canvas with a thick white sole. I agreed to send him a pair, which turned out to be classic canvas pumps. I sent them off a week after I arrived home but didn't hear whether he had got them or not. I would have loved to stay in touch with Marko and often wonder how he and Mina survived the war.

Last holiday reminiscences, honest. We first went to Barbados in the late Nineties and promptly fell in love with the place. The beaches, the people, and the climate are all wonderful and we have been lucky enough to have been able to visit almost every year since. The horsey set in Cheshire is quite a close group; the Cheshire Polo Club ground is only a mile or so from my house and I have been asked to exercise a few polo ponies during my riding years. Because of this connection, I have got to know some of the people who are involved with the club, and was amazed to learn that the club went over each year to play matches in Barbados. Watching polo both in Barbados and at the Cheshire ground is free for the majority of the matches. I have spent many a happy afternoon sitting by my car watching this great spectator sport. Drink is involved for the spectators and if you can ignore the very loud swearing coming from the field of play, a snooze in the sun can be a perfect way to spend a Sunday afternoon. I would recommend it. Back to holidays in Barbados. Last year (2016), our usual visit was dominated by illness; we both developed bad colds and I had trouble with my breathing so a visit to the doctor was called for. This involved walking twenty yards to a doctor's surgery and waiting your turn, no appointments required. After only ten minutes I was called in to see the very nice doctor and, after a long discussion on the West Indies versus England cricket match currently going on, I was diagnosed as having a chest infection, given suitable medication, charged forty Barbadian dollars, and happily sent on my way with the strict warning not to drink alcohol. Now, this was a real double blow. I was on my main holiday of the year and liked a glass of wine or two at dinner, but the even more annoying thing was that the hotel was fully inclusive of all drinks. Not entirely over my cold and the teetotal regime, a few days later I broke a tooth! This involved the same routine: find a dentist, wait your turn, and have your tooth fixed. A taxi took me to a dentist's surgery recommended by the hotel receptionist, but as I went in, I was not prepared for the loud reggae music belting out over the Tannoy system. Now, at this stage my imagination was running wild. I was thinking primitive methods, old-style instruments, and a huge muscular dentist for pulling teeth. How totally wrong can you be? The dentist was a very pretty young lady who looked about fifteen, but the surgery was state-of-the-art. The procedure was carried out without any pain and I was charged thirty Barbadian dollars and sent on my way. The taxi both ways cost more than the dentist's bill, but I returned to the hotel a happy man.

This short item is a follow-up to the last paragraph because it concerns medical facilities abroad and is in no way a travel piece...well, it is really, but it does contain medical information. We have spent many years travelling to Mallorca; in fact, our first visit to the island was on a short three-night break just after we met up, but most of our recent stays have been to Cala Millor, staying at the apartment of our sadly departed close friends, Val and Alan Pugh. We thought that when the apartment was sold that would be that, but on our last trip we learnt that the apartment had been sold to our good friends Steve and Susie Winter. Steve runs the complex and lives in one of the other apartments and has promised that we can continue to stay next year. Now for the promised medical bit. During our recent stay, Linda became unwell, and as a precaution I thought I had better get her to a doctor, but this was five thirty in the morning. A phone call to Susie not only gave us the information that a 24-hour medical clinic was a few kilometres away, but the insistence to drive us there. The clinic (in Son Servera) is a brand-new facility with free parking right outside, a nurse and doctor who speak good English, and, with the EU health card, comes at no cost. The clinic was empty, and Linda was seen in minutes and thankfully pronounced okay. As we were leaving, some twenty minutes after we arrived, Steve pulled up in the carpark asking if he could be of any help. You can't put a price on friends like that and we will be eternally grateful for their help and friendship.

Our NHS is a wonderful organisation, but if a small town in Mallorca can provide this sort of service, why can't we?

*A good deal all round.*

*Are those outfits for real?*

\*\*\*

# Chapter 19

## *Delamere Park*

When I was accepted for the Immigration Service, Linda and I were living in Handbridge, the other side of the River Dee from Chester, in a small block of apartments called Powell's Orchard. Living so close to Chester was one of the happiest times in a lifetime of happy times. On Saturday we would walk beside the Dee to Chester and have lunch and a spot of shopping. During that time, the very upmarket hotel The Grosvenor in the centre of the city had an all-you-can-eat buffet which was extremely reasonably priced, and we would really get our money's worth. It was also great to be able to have a meal or drinks in the evening and not have to drive home, but when I was working at Manchester Airport the journey became too much and I obtained a Crown transfer to Delamere Park.

When we first looked at the newly built houses on Delamere Park, we had the choice of three in our price range and we chose Hollow Oak Lane, which at that time looked out onto fields with cows grazing. However, there was an obstacle to overcome before we could buy the small two-bedroom house, and that was in the shape of the formidable letting agent, Mrs Johnson. Mrs Johnson had standards and wasn't going to let just anybody buy one of "her" houses. Before she agreed to let us look around the house we had taken a fancy to, we had to undergo an interview and came close to being rejected by Mrs Johnson. We were not married, and Mrs J. only considered married couples, but by telling her that a marriage was imminent, she agreed to "let us buy the property". We married twenty-eight years later! I was witness to Mrs Johnson's principles a little time later when I heard her inform a nice Asian man that all the remaining properties had been sold—not true. I shudder to think what she would have said in today's world, and indeed what the builders would have thought.

Life on Delamere Park in the early days was great. The concept was and still is an estate built around a clubhouse with a bar, swimming pool, and squash and tennis courts. All these facilities made for a very sociable life and as Linda played tennis at a high level and I dabbled in squash, we got to know most of the residents. There were also a lot of functions in the clubhouse such as the Christmas and New Year's Eve parties, so we had lots of friends, some of whom still live here after over forty years.

An event that ran for a few years on the park was one based on a TV series at the time called *Superstars*. This involved a series of sporting disciplines such as running and swimming, etc. The social committee put together a list of sporting disciplines appropriate to our facilities and invited residents to take part. The events included tennis, squash, running one lap of the estate (about one mile), swimming ten lengths of the pool (it's a very small pool), and the most sit-ups in a minute. It was all supposed to be fun but a lot of the people taking part were go-getting professionals and highly competitive. I entered knowing I hadn't a chance of winning as I couldn't play tennis, was very poor at squash, and running was never my forte, but I had high hopes of the swimming. I went on to win that event and, much to my great surprise, also came first in the sit-ups, but I must confess that the lad doing the counting was the son of our good friends, the Fitzsimmons, so he may have miss-counted a wee bit! I was very pleased to be in the top three, but to my shame never questioned my score in the sit-ups—thanks, Richard.

One of the couples living on the estate that we became very good friends with were Steve Coppell, the Manchester and England footballer, and his wife Jane, and we had many a happy night out with them. After Steve's playing career came to an end through injury and he became the manager of Crystal Palace, we lost touch somewhat, but still exchange Christmas cards every year. Steve is one of the nicest guys you could meet, and had his playing career not been halted he would have gone on to be one of our great English players. The other celebrity living on the estate at the time was Bob Carolgees, the TV presenter and host. Known for his glove puppet Spit the Dog, he and his wife were part of the social scene at Delamere Park in the Seventies and Eighties.

As I have said, one of the great benefits of living on Delamere Park was and in fact is still true today: the social life. As far as I can remember there was only the one fancy dress party held on the estate and, much against my better judgement, we attended. Linda looked gorgeous dressed as a bunny girl, and I, not wanting to spend much cash, went as the Incredible Hulk (expenditure: one tube of green face paint and an old torn shirt). Imagine my horror when we got to the clubhouse to find that only a very few residents had been told it was a fancy dress do, and that we were only one of four couples to have turned up in costume. To add insult to injury, the green paint didn't quite come off in one go, and I wandered around with a distinctive green pallor for the next few days.

The move to Delamere Park was one of the best decisions we ever made and even if that big lottery win came our way,

I would still continue to live here, but perhaps in one of the bigger houses. Delamere House and Delamere Park go back over two hundred years to the eighteenth century when the house was built by the Wilbraham family. During World War II, the estate became an army transit camp with British and American troops stationed there. It's rumoured that General Patton came here to address the troops before the D-Day landings. After the war, it became a home for displaced persons, mainly Polish, and when we first moved to the park there was still a Polish gentleman living in an old caravan near the estate, locally known as Joe the Pole. Joe attended, as a guest, some of the functions at the clubhouse, where he was bought many rounds of drinks. The sight of Joe, resplendent in wellies and an old overcoat, dancing with some of the ladies of the Park, was a sight to behold.

If you were to mention the name Barlow to most of the older residents on the estate, they would probably think you were talking about our lovely builder, Ian, who was a resident himself not so long ago. But if the same name was spoken to the younger residents, they would automatically think you were talking about Ian's younger brother, Gary. Gary, of course one of the country's leading singer-songwriters, was born in Frodsham, not far from Delamere, and for a few years lived in a palatial house a short way from the estate. When he lived there, you had to be particularly careful driving past the house as hordes of young fans were usually found camped outside the house and had a habit of trying to see if any passing car held their hero.

We have been lucky enough to have had some lovely and interesting neighbours on Delamere Park, not least Robert Lindsay and his wife Margaret. Bob is retired from the newspaper business where he was one of Robert Maxwell's directors. On the printing side of the industry, Bob has worked all over the world, and his tales of Maxwell and working for him are extremely entertaining and astonishing. Unfortunately, the libel laws of the UK prevent me from disclosing those tales. Being blessed with great neighbours, that's true of the present day as well as the past, is one of the main reasons we are still here after forty-three years. On the top of that list of lovely people are Frances Ryder and Bob Eagle. Over many years we have been lucky enough to be invited by them to spend a holiday with them at their beautiful house in New Zealand and for many lovely meals out. The most memorable has to be when Bob took us to his dining club, Mosimann's, in London. Mosimann's is a private member dining club and, since opening its doors in 1988, has entertained royalty from over a dozen different countries. Located in the heart of Belgravia and previously a Presbyterian church, it is one of the most prestigious private dining clubs in the world. The décor, the ambiance, and, of course, the food, were out of this world. One of the best meals I have ever had.

When we moved onto Delamere Park, some of our first visitors were my parents, who drove down from Northumberland with my mother's brother and his wife, my uncle, Fred, and aunt, Vi. I couldn't believe it when they told me of their journey down. They had driven the 200 odd miles on the motorways, and decided to stop to eat their sandwiches before continuing. My dad said that when Fred, who was driving, left the motorway, he went around the roundabout the wrong way and then stopped on wrong side of the short dual carriageway to have their lunch. They confessed that they didn't really know that at this point they were only seven miles from my house. Luckily, the A49 in those days was a much quieter road.

For many years now, a regular annual visitor to stay with us is my father-in-law, Ernest William Alfred Webb. Ernie has had quite a number of different jobs himself, serving in submarines during the war and with the London Transport Police, but for most of his working life as a Prison Officer in the Scottish Prison service. Ernie, in fact, reached the highest rank attainable in the service, that of Chief Principal Officer. When I was introduced to my future father-in-law and we talked for the first time, he told me that he had served in U-boats during the war. Not wanting to upset my future wife, I stayed silent, but for a long time I wondered which side he had been on. It later transpired that he was talking about the U-class of submarine and he didn't speak a word of German after all. Although born in London, he has lived in Scotland for most of his ninety-one years, and being a prison officer, I naturally called him "Fulton" after the actor who played Mr Mackay in the TV series *Porridge*. I often talked about Ernie to friends and workmates, and he would be astonished to hear how many people he had never met asked me, "How's Fulton?". As an Immigration Officer, I was required at times to interview people in prison and hated doing so, so I wasn't that keen when Fulton invited me on a tour of Inverness Prison where he was the Chief Officer at the time. However, I was amazed and impressed with the orderly way the inmates went about and the respect they seemed to show my father-in-law. This just didn't happen in my experience in England. One prison that I really didn't like visiting was Styal Woman's Prison where, if your escort was distracted, you were in danger of having your bum pinched. To get back to Fulton, he had an ambition to draw his prison pension for longer than he was paid a wage and he has achieved it this year, retiring at aged fifty-seven after thirty-three years' service, he is now aged ninety-one and has been retired for thirty-four years. He was awarded the British Empire Medal for meritorious civil service, worthy of recognition by the Crown, just before he retired.

Today, life on the park, or the camp as it was known to some of our neighbours, goes on. There are still functions and parties, the Guy Fawkes bonfire and firework display, the Christmas party, and the garden safaris, where some of the residents open their gardens and for a small fee you can buy a map of which gardens to see. One recent very successful addition to the social calendar is the themed dinners held in the clubhouse. These are extremely well supported, and we have only managed to get tickets to two, an Italian opera night and a Thai evening. All the meals are prepared by local restaurants and the entertainment is by the appropriate artists. Mostly supported by the older residents, they are a great opportunity to get together with friends on the park that you perhaps haven't seen for years, as well as being a really good evening. Delamere Park has played a big part in my life and I feel very lucky to have lived here.

*Linda showing off some of her trophies.*

*Not looking well at all.*

\*\*\*

# Chapter 20

## *Conclusion*

Life today seems to consist of trying to keep oneself alive and fit enough to travel on yet another holiday or short break away. With this in mind, I have been a member of a gym for over forty years, which isn't borne out by my present shape or size. I also seem to have been on one diet or another for all of those years, and dread to think what size I would be had I not tried to control my weight. I think I may have a very slow metabolism. No—I just love good food! I used to have a General Practitioner who was almost twice my size, and never once did she make any comments about my weight, but my present GP looks to be eight stone ringing wet and never stops reminding me of the dangers of being "full-sized". Whatever happened to the idea of being "fat but fit"?

Looking back, I have had a good life and an interesting one. I seem to have had more jobs (can't call them careers) than most, and I think that I have seen more places than the average man in the street. I have been extremely lucky to have had my wife, Linda, all these years. I know that I haven't made much of a mark in this world; there are no blue plaques on buildings showing I lived there. I sometimes fantasize that the daughter I only saw at a few days old grew up to have children of her own, and that one of my grandchildren is on the point of discovering a cure for cancer. Now, that would be something. I have thoroughly enjoyed putting this all down on paper, and in doing so, it has brought back fond memories of places and people long passed and not thought about for many years. When one thinks about it, being thought of when you're no longer here is the best that most of us can hope for. The only purpose of this book was to put a small marker down to show I did exist, and hopefully put a wry smile on one or two faces after I've gone. As to the reasons for writing this memoir, I may be stating the obvious again, but I have written this for myself and, as stated, have had an enormous amount of pleasure in doing so. I'm sure that some will say it's badly written, boring in parts, and self-indulgent in the extreme. That's as may be; I don't care. Of course, there are certain aspects of my life I would have done differently, but to end with a dreadful cliché: I did it my way. If I have learnt anything in this life, it's to live life every day, try not to hurt anyone, stay healthy, and don't waste whatever talents you may have been blessed with. If you are reading this, you're already far more fortunate than all the friends and colleagues that are no longer with us. Be grateful and enjoy life.

*In my own kitchen, where I can be found most evenings.*

*** The End ***

#0171 - 270418 - C0 - 229/152/12 - PB - DID2183359